The SINCLAIR ZX81
Programming for Real Applications

The SINCLAIR ZX81

Programming for Real Applications

Randle Hurley

dilithium Press

First edition 1981
Reprinted 1981, 1982

Published by
THE MACMILLAN PRESS LTD
London and Basingstoke

First published in the USA 1982

Printed in the USA

ISBN 0–88056–090–8

dilithium Press
P.O. Box 606
Beaverton, Oregon 97075

Contents

I would like to express my gratitude to all the ZX80 and ZX81 enthusiasts who have contributed towards this book. Some made their contributions directly but the majority will probably be oblivious of having helped. During countless conversations centring round the machines, chance remarks have sparked off the ideas which led to the finished programs in this work. Steve Adams made many of the direct contributions and his idea on modifying the 3K RAM pack is included in the chapter on hardware. However you made your contribution, thanks.

Particular thanks must go to my wife, Linda. The original idea was that she should read and criticise the material from a complete beginner's point of view but she learned so fast that she became the major bug finder and editor as well. Thanks, love, I couldn't have got half way through without you.

1 Aims and Assumptions

When I sat down first to work my material into a book I had to make some assumptions about the sort of reader that I was writing for. The person that I had in mind when writing was not a computer expert. My target reader had finished all the material in the Sinclair manual and probably did not really understand those bits about Procrustean Assignment and Unary Functions. He or she will probably have read a book or two of games programs and perhaps will have been interested in some of the ideas presented in the pages of magazines devoted to the ZX81. My reader may have shared my frustration that these ideas, while fascinating, are given in isolation and seldom related to any real task the ZX81 may be called on to do. The person I am writing for may be a teacher like myself, hoping to use their machine for academic organisation or as an educational tool. On the other hand, I may be writing for someone interested in using the ZX81 to help run a small business or a social club. All these possible needs have been borne in mind during the writing.

The program listings shown in these chapters not only work, they are workhorses, doing real jobs in a variety of environments. Each of the ideas presented has been followed through to a real conclusion and not used simply to illustrate a nice programming point. Lack of finance for a larger machine meant that the ZX81 simply had to do my data processing work. Necessity forced me to consider alternative ways of using the ZX81's BASIC and these alternatives have proved to be very useful. None of the ideas used in the programs shown is highly technical and so they will all be quite easy for even a relatively inexperienced programmer to understand. Expect to find a logical extension of the material in the handbook and some interesting twists in the way that it has been put to work.

While we are still on the subject of assumptions, I have assumed that the reader has a fully expanded machine. Some of the programs occupy the whole of the 16K RAM pack and all of them are too big for the 1K ZX81. The ZX printer has been considered and commands for it have been written into some of the programs. In all but one case the programs will work satisfactorily without this extra. The word processing package, however, really does rely on the availability of a printer for most of its uses. Towards the end you will find a chapter on some simple hardware modifications. Anyone who has built the kit will find no difficulty in making the modifications but, while they more than repay the small amount of work involved, these are in no way necessary for the smooth running of the programs.

Games programs teach a lot about how the computer works and about the facilities available on the machine but even the most avid games player will eventually tire of the material on offer and will look for alternatives. And then there are those awkward people who keep on asking the classic question: "that's interesting, but what is it for?" A glance through the contents of the book will be enough to provide several answers to the askers of this question and at the same time dispute the idea that the ZX81 is a toy computer, suitable only for keeping the children quiet on wet afternoons and for drilling them in their arithmetic. The central processor of the ZX81 is the same Z80A chip found in many, much larger machines which run commercial organisations. If this chip can run a wages and stock control system or a word processor when built into other computers then there must be a lot of untapped potential in the ZX81 and my aim has been to exploit this. I hope that those readers who have tired of the normal diet offered to ZX81 users will share in the great satisfaction that I have had from coaxing the little machine to take on tasks normally thought to demand a much larger computer.

A quick flip through the pages which follow might give the impression that the contents are much the same as to be found in all the other books of programs; large chunks of not very inteligible code and hardly the thing for someone who has just closed the pages of the handbook for the first time.

Well, look again. The chunks are all quite small, seldom more than about ten lines. The reader has very little to key into the machine at any one time and the likelihood of a line being missed from a long listing is reduced considerably. Now look closer still. All the code is accompanied by little bits in English. Every line which is the slightest bit difficult to understand is explained there and then. Readers are not expected to have infallible memories, if the same idea crops up in a later line then the explanation is given again. The information in English that accompanies the code, the documentation, is not limited to explaining the hard bits. All the GO TO instructions are accompanied by notes on the material to be found at the line that the computer is to jump to. GO SUB lines carry reminders of what it is that each subroutine does. On the occasions that PEEK and POKE commands are used, information on the identity of the value being "peeked at" and the purpose of the number being "poked" is given in full. Where the logical structure of the program is spread over a large number of lines and is difficult to grasp as a whole then the explanatory notes are supplemented by a flow chart.

The first chapter after this introduction is on programming. This is not intended to be a course in BASIC. It is a supplement to the handbook material and looks at ways of making the fullest possible use of the ZX81 facilities. In places, this chapter reads a little like a list of household tips. Even such small matters as the type of exercise books to consider and the benefits of shelf lining paper are covered. Later, the cost of all the commands and the functions is investigated in terms of both memory use and running time. These investigations are built up into some general observations on programming the ZX81 more effectively.

The main aim of the book is to develop in the reader an interest in pushing the ZX81 computer much further than anyone expected it to go when it was first launched. The programs will show you how to store more numbers than there are memory bytes in the 16K machine *and* then access this idea in many different ways afterwards. You will find the necessary information on how to reduce the likelihood of your programs crashing the moment they are handed over to an inexperienced user. Ways of storing large amounts of text which remain available for editing and ways of storing numbers as text to improve storage efficiency will be made available to you. More important than all this, however, after reading the material you should have discarded the belief that the ZX81 is too small for any real computing work. The programs given here are just the beginning; the techniques are flexible enough to be worked into your own programs to fill your own data processing needs.

The material can be approached at two levels. On the one hand, there are large, powerful, "off the peg" programs which can be put to work at once or modified to suit particular needs. Alternatively, you can use the programs as working examples to illustrate the programming ideas given in the early part of the book. The ideas and the examples can then be used as a basis for the development of entirely new and different programs for completely different applications. I hope that most readers will approach the material from both angles at different times. Teachers, by the way, may find ideas of interest in the non-educational programs and I hope that those of you without an involvement in education will enjoy the programming ideas in the educational material.

2 *Programming*

Although the ZX81 can now be expanded to 64K and more of user RAM, by the use of one of a number of add-on RAM units, this is still quite expensive. The 16K limit can be seen as a restriction on programming style or, more optimistically, as a valuable spur to improve the effective use of the space available. The material in this chapter is concerned with the development of an approach to the programming task which suits the machine we are working with. It is not intended as a course in BASIC.

The 16K of memory is not all that small. It would be a hefty program, indeed, which would occupy the whole memory. The size of the RAM is limiting because it is not only the program which has to live there, all the data which the program is designed to process has to use this space as well. In larger systems, the data is often held in files on tape or disc and is loaded into the computer during the run so the whole of the information does not have to be held in RAM at one time. As the data is used and perhaps modified, it can be dumped back on to the tape or disc to make room for the next batch. The ideas which follow are designed to help in the organisation of the space we have. They may be used as a check list. Mentally tick off those habits that you use in your programming already. You may wish to consider the items that remain for inclusion in your tool kit of programming techniques.

The first thing to organise is the paper on which the program is to be planned and written. The programs under discussion in this book are not the sort which can be written at the keyboard, straight off from line 10 to line 1500, pausing only for a cup of coffee at line 750. Large programs like these have to be planned out in advance because ordinary mortals cannot hold all the ideas in their heads, translate them into code and organise the code into a logical structure, all at the same time. A 20p exercise book is a worthwhile investment for each major program. The type of exercise book with squared paper, sometimes referred to as "quadrille" often has thirty-two lines to the page. It might be necessary to rule in the last couple in the space left at the top of the page. Quadrille is particularly suitable because it matches the thirty-two character to the line format of the ZX81. Whichever type of exercise book you choose, the whole of the programming process can be organised between its covers and at the end you will have automatically documented the finished program. A set of these exercise books can be neatly filed away and the likelihood of the information being thrown away by mistake is less than it would be if the material were written on a collection of tatty pieces of paper.

The writing of the lines of BASIC should be put off for quite a time. The first thing is to break down the job to be programmed into chunks which are small enough to be translated into code at one go. Use a couple of pages at the front of the exercise book to write down a brief description of these chunks. Space out the list well to allow for the insertion of a forgotten section. As programming proceeds, the sections can be crossed off as they are covered. In this way no section of the job should be neglected.

On the next double page, draw up a chart for the variables that will be used in the program. It is all to easy to forget that "G" has been used to store the number of goals scored in a game program and use the same variable to record the number of goes the player has had since the run began. Once a variable has been set up it will remain in the area of the memory called the variables store until it is reset or the commands RUN or CLEAR are used. The more variables that are set up the more memory will be booked and the longer the loading and saving time will be. All the variables are saved onto the tape as well as the program. The chart allows you to organise your variables and set up as few as possible. If an input is trivial, a selection from a menu for instance, then the information need not be stored. Such information may be fed into variables "A" and A$ and these two can be permanently booked in your chart for such jobs. All data of more lasting interest can be fed into other variables and noted down in the chart as they are set. The ZX80/81 User's Club have proposed some programming standards which it might be as well to consider here. It is suggested that the variables start at "A" and follow through in single letters, in alphabetical order. The recommendation is that you avoid using the letters "O", "I", "S" and "Z" as variable names because these are so easily confused with the numbers 0, 1, 2 and 5. One final suggestion from the guidelines is that a space in a string of characters be shown as " * " except where there are a lot of spaces when the preferred method of representation would be: " 17 spaces ". The User's Club suggest these as guidelines and not rules and I have adopted them as such because they seem to make a lot of sense and are simple to follow.

Having broken down the job into its component parts you will probably have some ideas on how to code these sections into BASIC so now is the time to start writing the program. Start at the back of the exercise book; some ideas are bound not to work and several attempts might have to be made before a working solution is found. Keep the front of the book for the fair copy and hide away the mistakes at the back. Before moving away from the variables chart it is necessary to consider the special case of those variables which act as counters in FOR/NEXT loops. Here, again, some counters can be used over and over while others must be set aside for one special job. Mathematicians tend to use the counter "I" for loops because it stands for "integer" but this conflicts with the guidelines mentioned earlier. My own preference is to use "J", "K" and "L" as loop counters and I have seldom had to use more than three counters in one program.

When a loop runs straight through and there is no possibility of jumping out to another area of the program while it is cycling, then the value of the counter is of no importance when the loop is completed. All such loops can share the same counter. It might be thought useful to jump out of a loop half way through and go to a different part of the job for a while before returning. In this case, the value of the loop counter must not be altered and it would be wise to allocate a special variable for this loop. It is worth pointing out that the ZX81 will remember the state of all loop counters even when the program is saved onto tape. The counters are printed to the tape in the same way that all the other variables are. If a great deal of data has to be entered and there is only time to enter some of it then the loop can be left, the program stored, loaded at a later date and the loop will start up again in the same place as if you had never been away from the keyboard. This facility is used in one of the programs listed later.

STRUCTURING THE WRITING OF THE PROGRAM

If the job that the ZX81 has to do has subsections, then it might be helpful if this fact was reflected in the structure of the written program. If the first section were to start at line 1000 and the second at line 2000 and so on then the part of the program on the screen at any time can be easily related to the overall plan. We might not be too well off for memory with the ZX81 but we have 9999 line numbers available to us and at a minimum cost of six memory bytes per line, we cannot possibly use all of them. If we have to be so careful with memory it might do us good to spend line numbers a little more freely. Before the main meat of the code starts at each step of 1000 lines, insert a CLS (clear screen) line. This will automatically clear away unwanted display from the previous section and is good housekeeping.

SUBROUTINES

The subroutines can go anywhere in the program but some places have definite advantages. Each routine has to be by-passed until it is called and a GO TO line is needed. If the subroutines are all together then one GO TO line will by-pass the lot. The routines can go at the beginning, in the middle or at the end. The beginning has a small advantage in that the command GO TO 9000 costs two more memory bytes than GO TO 60. This is a small saving but costs nothing more than the effort to develop a programming habit. In programs which make heavy use of sub-routines these small savings can add up to a large memory saving.

ARITHMETIC PROBLEMS

Compared with the ZX80 with its arithmetic limit of 32 767, the ZX81 is pretty safe from the problem of arithmetic overflow. There are few programs which require the machine to cope with numbers in excess of 10^{38}. The ZX81 is not completely immune from arithmetic overflow, for it can happen by mistake when a number is divided by zero or a very small number. This results in the machine trying to represent infinity, giving up, and displaying the error code 6/ . Asking the machine to perform the impossible such as finding the square root of a negative number generates an error code A/ . Whenever an error code is generated the program will stop running. The programmer will know that all that is needed in many cases is to key CONT and the machine will recover - but the programs may be intended for less experienced users than the programmer. When there is a possibility that such arithmetic problems might arise, then your program will have to recognise the trouble before the central processor does and shuts down the run.

FLOW CHARTS

Now that you have started writing the code that represents the programming ideas you have had, you are bound to have problems. It is unlikely that the first idea that you try will always work and you may have to discard it and try a fresh approach. With a difficult logic problem you may find that you are attacking the problem in many different ways and getting no nearer to a solution. It is time to fall back onto flow charting. The purists would say that we should have started from the flow chart in the first place! It is surprising, once you master the art of chart construction, how the solution to a difficult logic problem emerges quite painlessly from a flow diagram. The same problem may not have responded to a whole evening spent at the computer trying the more direct route.

A flow charting stencil is not essential but it does help keep the whole thing neat and tidy. After all, logic problems do seem to respond best to an orderly approach. Stencils are difficult to get hold of and are ridiculously expensive. You may well find yourself having to pay more for your small piece of plastic than you had to pay for this book. The simpler ones are cheaper and as long as it has the following outlines, buy the cheapest one you can find.

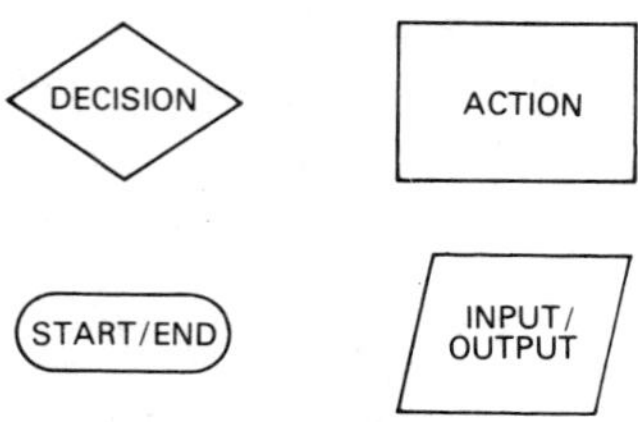

A good quality stencil will have rounded edges which allow the representation of smooth data flow:

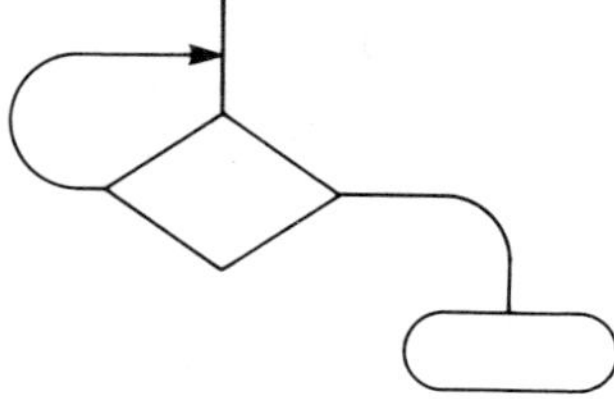

It will also have lines printed on it which allow the outlines to be lined up precisely with previously drawn shapes.

The technique of flow charting is best acquired by experience but many would-be chart constructors find getting started difficult. It often helps to draw out the chart of a logic problem that has already been programmed. A simple problem to get your teeth into is the input check routine which you will find at the bottom of page 11. Start with the main question at line 1010:

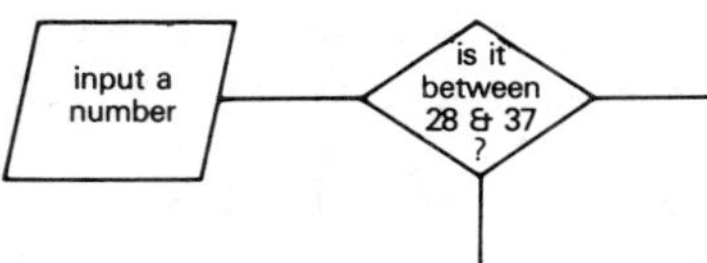

Draw out the chart to represent the program segment including the subroutine at line 2000. This is where the shelf lining paper, mentioned in the introduction, comes into the limelight. This paper comes in long rolls about two feet wide and can be cut up into convenient lengths for flow charting. Once you become experienced with charts you won't need all that space but, at first, if you start your chart right in the middle of an enormous piece of paper you can wander round it as much as you need to before you find the path that does the job you need doing.

CHECKING THE INPUT FOR MISTAKES

It is essential that frequent opportunities are given to check any input from the keyboard before it is irrevocably accepted by the computer. If large amounts of data have to be keyed in then mistakes will happen. If only one opportunity to check your typing is given during the feeding in of twenty pieces of information and the first one is wrong, then the rest will have to be entered, rejected along with the mistake and then keyed in again. Secondly, a single mistake in twenty pieces is less easy to spot than one amongst five, and may be overlooked.

Computer users are not very good input devices, as people in general are rather unreliable. We need variety in the tasks that we are expected to do, unlike other methods of feeding in data. We cannot go on all day without making mistakes. We are mesmerised by repetitive tasks and need frequent changes to keep our accuracy high. One change which helps add variety to the task of feeding in data is checking the material that has been entered. To make the most of this change of task, a new style of presentation of the data should be adopted. If the figures were printed horizontally at first, they could be presented vertically for checking. If this is not possible then call attention to the fact that the checking time has come round again by printing a suitable message in inverse graphics. Inverse graphics, by the way, look much better if they are preceded and followed by an inverse space.

My own optimum number of pieces of information to be keyed in before the next checking routine is five. If there are fewer than fifty entries required then I can cope with ten or more without making too many typing errors. If data has to be loaded into an array then the checking routine could be something like:

```
10      FOR J = 1 TO 20
20      PRINT " KEY THE VALUE OF ITEM * " ; J
30      INPUT A(J)
40      NEXT J
50      PRINT " KEY M FOR A MISTAKE OR C FOR CORRECT "
60      INPUT A$
70      IF A$ <> " C " THEN GO TO 10
```

It is important to point out that the user needs to do something active to signal a correct set of data. The more passive " KEY M FOR MISTAKE OTHERWISE NEWLINE " is likely to lead to errors because users become so used to having to press NEWLINE that it becomes an automatic response even when it ought to be preceded by "M".

Instead of having a check routine at every point in the program where input is called for, the check can be made more general in character and programmed as a subroutine to be called after each set of data is fed in.

Commercial systems designed to be as robust as possible often have more memory devoted to checking the input to prevent crashes and to eliminate data which is obviously wrong, than is devoted to doing the job the system is designed for. One educational program is interesting in this regard. It invites students to spell a word which was part of a screenful of text displayed earlier. Incorrect spellings gradually switch in more and more input protection routines which reject more and more of the incorrect spellings until, eventually the computer will not respond to any keystrokes unless they are the correct letters in the right order. The program is remarkably effective at helping low ability students with their spellings.

Because we are limited to a small amount of memory on the ZX81, we cannot expect to protect our programs against all inappropriate forms of input and so some crashes are bound to occur. If every keystroke which could wreck a program were to be guarded against, the programs would run very slowly and we would be limited to the very simple programs that would fit into the small space left. A balance has to be struck; it is prudent to protect your work against the more likely errors but foolish to try to cope with all possible mistakes.

There are various ways of getting information into the machine and all of them have their problems. If your program has a line:

```
1000   INPUT A
```

then any input which is not made up entirely of figures or which includes more than one decimal point will give an error code and stop the run. The user will not know about the use of the CONTinue command unless he or she happens to be relatively experienced at working the machine.

The line: 1000   INPUT A$, is much more forgiving. It will cause the ZX81 to accept any input from the keyboard. The input may be accepted at this stage but still cause problems later. If a single digit is all that is required from the operator then the number can be generated from the character by finding the CODE of the string. The code of each number character is twenty-eight more than its value so if this amount is subtracted from the code, there is your number. Number characters have codes inside the range, 28 to 37 and a simple addition to the program eliminates all the other characters.

```
1000   INPUT A$
1010   IF CODE A$ < 28 OR CODE A$ > 37 THEN GO TO 1000
1020   LET A = CODE A$ - 28
```

Users, however, will not expect the machine to ignore information and may not even notice that it has done so. It would be better to draw the user's attention to the fact that the input was not suitable. The way that is chosen must be friendly or, at the very least, polite. Too many have been put off the whole idea of computing because all attempts to communicate with the machine are met with "input error", "what" or even worse a report code such as the ZX81 generates; B/1165. User friendliness is expensive: in computing it does cost something to be polite! In spite of the high cost these systems which help new users use the programs are essential. Try something like this general purpose, input rejection subroutine:

```
1010   IF A < 28 OR A > 37 THEN GO SUB 2000
1020   IF A < 28 OR A > 37 THEN GO TO 1000
```

and at 2000:

```
2000   PRINT " I CANNOT COPE WITH THE INFORMATION IN THIS
FORM. PLEASE TRY AGAIN OR GET HELP "
```

```
2010   FOR J = 1 TO 200  }   delay loop long enough
2020   NEXT J            }   to allow reading
2030   CLS
2040   RETURN
```

Another way of getting numerical input into the machine is to use the ZX81's VAL function on a string of characters. This returns the numerical value of the whole string whereas the CODE technique only looks at the first character. If a mixture of numbers and letters were entered then VAL would cause an error report. Inexperienced users often use "O", the letter, in place of zero. On the whole, VAL is not much use in this situation and a more robust method of sorting out the input must be found.

The following routine is twenty-five lines long and a little expensive in memory bytes but it will accept anything from the keyboard and give a polite message about any invalid keystrokes. Read the listing in conjunction with these notes:

Line 20 simply rejects the NEWLINE key used alone.

Lines 30 and 40 measure the length of the string and set up temporary storage for the characters which make it up.

50 resets a flag which holds the position of the decimal point.

Lines 60 to 120 form a loop which cycles as many times as there are characters in the string.

Line 80 rejects all characters except figures. It also rejects the decimal point if there are more than one in the figure. "X" is set to the position of the decimal point in the string so if "X" is not equal to zero then there must be two points in the string.

Line 90 sets "X" to the position of the point.

Line 100 loads the value (the CODE less 28) into the correct element of the array set up at line 40.

Line 110 removes the leading character of the string so that, next time around, the CODE of the next character is read.

Line 130 resets A for a second job.

Line 140 adds a decimal point to a number keyed in without one. The point is added at the end.

Lines 150 to 180 form a second loop which cycles as many times as the first one did.

Lines 160 and 170 extract from the array the digits which made up the original number. If J equals X then this element holds the decimal point and so is ignored. The separate digits are multiplied or divided by ten as many times as necessary to restore each to the value it had in the original number. The values are then added to regenerate the number.

Lines 210 to 250 are kept out of the main loop because they are only needed occasionally. If they were to be kept in the loop it would run more slowly. As it is the routine takes about a second to register a three digit number in fast mode.

Line 230 checks for the presence of two decimal points and rejects the input if two are found.

The routine is safe but slow and is only to be recommended if few numbers are involved. It might be thought suitable for educational programs which are used with students who find difficulty with the keyboard.

CRASHPROOFING SUBROUTINE

```
10      INPUT A$
20      IF A$ = " " THEN GO TO 10
30      LET Y = LEN A$
40      DIM Z ( Y )
50      LET X = 0
60      FOR J = 1 TO Y
70      LET A = CODE A$
80      IF A < 27 OR A > 37 THEN GO TO 210
90      IF A = 27 THEN GO TO 230
100     LET Z(J) = A - 28
110     LET A$ = A$ ( 2 TO )
120     NEXT J
130     LET A = 0
140     IF X = 0 THEN LET X = Y + 1
150     FOR J = 1 TO Y
160     IF J > X THEN LET A = A + Z(J) * 10 ** ( X - J )
170     IF J < X THEN LET A = A + Z(J) * 10 ** ( X - J - 1 )
```

```
180     NEXT J
190     PRINT A
200     RETURN
210     PRINT "     suitable error message     "
220     GO TO 10
230     IF X <> 0 THEN GO TO 210
240     LET X = J
250     GO TO 110
```

The next type of input which needs attention is the response to a menu. If the input is in the form of a string, even though the menu invites a reply in number form, then any response will be accepted. All that remains is to cover the case of a reply that was not on offer on the screen. Imagine that the following list generated the reply "3":

```
10      PRINT " KEY 1 FOR EGGS "
20      PRINT " KEY 2 FOR BACON "
30      INPUT A$
40      IF A$ = " 1 " THEN GO TO 100
50      IF A$ = " 2 " THEN GO TO 200
100     REM   REST OF THE PROGRAM STARTS HERE
```

The result of keying "3" will be that the machine will select the action programmed at line 100. The result will be the same for all input except " 2 ". If, however, line 60 is added:

```
60      GO TO 10
```

then the action programmed at 100 would only be performed if " 1 " was keyed in. A better solution would be to call the earlier subroutine (page 11) to cope with inappropriate input, print a suitable message and then clear the screen before calling for the input again.

AUTO START UP

It is mildly annoying to have to key RUN/NEWLINE after a program has been loaded from the cassette. More important, if data has been previously loaded into the program, the use of RUN or CLEAR must be avoided or the information will disappear. One way of reducing the likelihood of RUN being used is to arrange the SAVE instruction as part of a series of lines like this:

```
5000    CLS
5010    SAVE " PROGRAM NAME "
5020    GO TO (where the computer needs to go when starting
                 again)
```

This results in the ZX81 going into the SAVE sequence when control is sent to line 5000. The last letter of the program name will be turned into an inverse video version of itself as a result of this system but this seems to have very little effect. When the program is loaded into the ZX81 again it will continue with the previous program run and start work at line 5020. As a consequence the program starts up automatically at the correct line without the use of RUN and the risk of losing all the precious variables.

The Auto Start Up routine makes the following suggestion reasonable. When RUN or CLEAR were stronger possibilities then this method of saving memory was not very safe. If these lines are included in a program:

```
10    DIM A ( 200 )
20    LET X = 16396
30    LET A$ = " THE QUICK RED FOX IS QUITE NICE REALLY "
```

Then the information is held in the memory twice. Once in the program area where it is stored as lines of program and again in the Variables Store where the space is set aside for the array, X is remembered and the ruddy fox is described. Why store this information twice when once would do? It is a simple matter to set up all these variables as commands, lines keyed in and entered without line numbers. Perhaps a safer approach if there are a lot of such variables to set up would be to enter these commands as lines. RUN the program to execute the instructions and then delete the lines to release the memory that they occupy.

A detailed approach to the task of saving memory and keeping an eye on the cost of programming methods is to be found in the next chapter "Saving Time and Space". The rest of this chapter will be devoted to debugging and documentation.

BUG-HUNTING

When the first of the chunks into which your task has been broken is programmed, run through the lines to see if the objective has been reached. Sometimes the first run through will not go as smoothly as you might wish. This will probably be because what you told the computer to do and what you thought you had told it were two different things. You have bugs. Bugs are nasty little errors in the program which have to be found and eliminated before the program will run exactly as required. Everybody has bugs and they are nothing to be ashamed of. The program which is built into the ZX81 ROM has a bug, its calculation of square roots is not quite mathematically perfect, so you are in good company. The ZX81 will give you some information which will help you to narrow down the area of the program which is at fault so you will not have to go through the whole list to find a tiny error.

The error code printed on the screen when a run has stopped due to a fault is the first source of help. The meaning of these reports is given in the manual on page 189. Look up the meaning of the first part of the report and find out what caused the problem. The next hint that the machine gives you is the line number in your program run where the problem was noticed. 2/1750 means that you have asked the ZX81 to use a variable but have not told it what the value of this variable is. The first time this variable crops up as the machine works through the program is at line 1750. Key in LIST, followed by the line number and most times the reason for the trouble will be obvious. If you are still puzzled about the reason for the aborted run then it is time to consider a "dry run". In programs of the complexity that we are considering, it is wise to organise a dry run before putting the machine to serious work even if the program seems to run faultlessly. A dry run is a manual run through the program on some simple data. The state of the variables is noted down at each stage of the process in a chart. The program is then treated to a supply of STOP lines at the end of each section. When the program is RUN, it will stop at the first STOP command at the end of the first section of code. The report code 9/line number, will appear on the screen. Give the ZX81 PRINT commands for all the variables which you have in your listing. The values that you have worked out by hand can then be compared with the values held in the computer. If "A" should equal 57 at the first stage and it prints as A = 0, then the bug in your program will be in the area of the code which calculates the value of "A".

Just because the program that you have written runs through and ends with a report code of 0/5000, it cannot be assumed that there are no bugs. The dry run is needed to check that the machine produces the right answers to the problems and that you have not given it some instructions which do a job which is very slightly different from the one you need doing. BASIC is quite like English but there are important differences. We can be a lot less precise in our choice of words in English than we can in BASIC and still convey our meaning. Take the following, for instance: "If a value is greater than the minimum allowed or less than the maximum allowed then it can be included". There are two problems here. Does the greater than and less than mentioned mean just what they say or is the value to be included in the list if it *equals* either the maximum or the minimum? The second problem is less easy to spot. Reading the English version of the statement with the imagination that we bring to most material we read, we assume that the value is to be included if it lies between the maximum and the minimum. In BASIC we can assume no imagination because computers have none. The innocent looking "OR" in the English statement will cause real trouble if it is not replaced by an AND when the line is translated into BASIC:

```
1000   IF VALUE <= MAX AND VALUE >= MIN THEN PRINT VALUE
```

Your program with the essential translation stage missing will work without error codes being printed but the result will not be as you expected. Dry runs are, therefore, essential where the programs are at all complex.

What if the problem still remains hidden after both these methods of identifying it have been tried? You could try asking a friend to look at the problem for you. A fresh approach to the problem, one which is not inextricably bound up with your assumptions about it, can often see through the difficulty very quickly. If there is still no solution then consider abandoning the approach that you have selected for this part of the job. There are usually several different ways in which a job can be done by the ZX81, try another one. Very often the solution to the difficulty you had with the first attempt will occur to you as soon as you have finished writing the section of code by the second method! Having found all the bugs and having proved that the ZX81 does the job that you intended it to do, don't forget to delete all those STOP lines. Don't despair if you keep getting bugs in your programs, everyone does. They tend to get fewer and less difficult to cure as you become more experienced but they never go away completely.

Once the program is under way and sections work without a hitch, start writing the fair copy in the front of your exercise book. This will be so much easier for those readers with an ZX printer but, whichever method you use to write your LIST, only use the left hand side of each double page. The documentation of the program goes on the right hand side. It might seem a little pointless, explaining the program lines that you, yourself, have written. The reason for documenting even those programs that will never be shown to anyone else is that it is surprising how quickly the code becomes difficult to understand. Lines may be baffling a few hours, let alone a few weeks, after you have written them. During the writing process you are bound up with the exact condition of a small piece of the program and each statement in each line is very clear in its meaning because you are so involved. As you move on to new lines and become involved with the minute detail of these, the command over the ideas used in the previous section lessens.

As you develop as a programmer you will not wish to re-work every job afresh when you have a section of code in a previous program which, with a minimum of modification, can be reused. Just think how frustrating it would be to spend hours working out how your earlier masterpiece actually worked when a few minutes spent writing up the lines in note form would save all the bother.

A final small point, related to programming if not to the material in this book. If a program has been written for the 1K machine and saved onto tape without the 16K RAM pack in place, then it will not load into an expanded ZX81. Similarly, when a program has been written on a 16K machine, even if it is small enough to have been written on a 1K machine, it will not load into the smaller computer. This point is worth bearing in mind if you are in the habit of developing small sections of the larger program on the un-expanded ZX81 and wish to load them into the larger version for further development. It took me a long time and a lot of frustration before I realised this simple fact.

SUMMARY

The organisation of the programming task has been discussed from two points of view. The organisation of the physical materials and the building up of the program in neat blocks was discussed from the point of view of increasing programming efficiency. The ZX81 Users Group recommendations on programming were examined briefly.

Amongst the points of detail that were dealt with were: management of loops, arithmetic problems, flow charting and input protection. A method of protecting the variables stored in a program from loss due to the use of RUN and CLEAR was given. This method is based on the "auto start-up" of programs. This means of starting the program automatically led, in turn, to a way of avoiding unnecessary memory use.

General de-bugging of programs and the "dry run" technique finished off the chapter.

3 Saving Time and Space

The ZX80 computer, fore-runner of the ZX81, could only cope with numbers up to 32 766 and down to minus 32 767. It could not deal with decimals and ignored everything that came after the decimal point. Despite its limitations, it had one or two advantages over the ZX81. It was much faster and it used its memory much more sparingly than the more recent machine. The ZX81 has to pay for its ability to cope with very large numbers and decimals in some way. The payment is made in speed and having to use a lot of memory. This chapter looks at ways of reducing the price we have to pay for the new facilities.

The ZX80 stored each of its numbers in two different memory stores, one after the other in the random access memory. Two of these stores, or bytes, were needed because the largest number that can be stored in one byte is 255. Any number was stored in the memory by dividing it by 256, storing the remainder in the first of the pair of bytes and then storing the result of the division in the second byte. The ZX80 regenerated its numbers by reversing this process, multiplying the value of the second byte by 256 and adding the contents of the first. To Store 1000:

divide 1000 by 256 result = 3 remainder = 232

store the remainder in the first byte of the pair

store the result in the second byte of the pair

The second byte has two jobs to do, hold the result of the division and also indicate whether the number is positive or negative. Some of its space is taken up with the sign of the number and so the most that can be held in the remaining space is 127. The ZX80 would reject any number which required the second byte to hold more than 127 and described the situation as "arithmetic overflow".

Try Storing 40 000

divide 40 000 by 256   result = 156   remainder = 64

store the remainder in the first byte of the pair

the result is more than 127 so report "arithmetic overflow"

Try Storing 32 767

divide 32 767 by 256   result = 127   remainder = 255

store the remainder in the first byte of the pair

store the result in the second byte of the pair

This is the largest number that can be stored using two memory bytes while still indicating a positive or negative number.

The ZX81 uses five of the memory stores for each number. The process of storage is the same but, because of the extra space, enormous numbers can be entered and used in calculations. This is how the five bytes are used:

Number / 256 = Result 1 + Remainder 1
store the remainder in the first byte

Result 1 / 256 = Result 2 + Remainder 2
store remainder 2 in the second byte

Result 2 / 256 = Result 3 + Remainder 3
store remainder 3 in the third byte

Result 3 / 256 = Result 4 + Remainder 4
store remainder 4 in the fourth byte

Check that result 4 is less than 128
if it is less than 128 store result 4 in byte 5
if it is more than 127 print arithmetic
overflow message and then stop.

Arithmetic overflow does not occur until a number larger than 1×10^{38} is entered or generated by the machine.

Just looking at the extra work that the computer has to do in storing numbers is enough to indicate that the ZX81 will be slower than a machine which uses only two bytes per number. The following program was tried on both machines to find out how the speed suffered as a result of the extra storage space:

```
10      FOR J = 1 TO 1000
20      LET A = 10 ** 2
```

```
30     NEXT J
40     PRINT " DONE "
```

and these times were recorded:

ZX80	4 seconds
ZX81 (fast mode)	1 minute 54 seconds
ZX81 (slow mode)	7 minutes 38 seconds

Obviously the manipulation of all those extra bytes takes the Z80 central processor a great deal of time. As well as keeping a close eye on the amount of memory being used while writing programs it will be necessary to consider how much time the work will take. Those readers who have become used to working on the ZX80 before moving on to the ZX81 may have developed programming habits which could lead to very long delays if they are not modified. The bulk of the material in this chapter is devoted to the cost of program lines but there are a few, valuable techniques which will save processing time as well.

Those readers who feel that they would like another go at understanding the way numbers are arranged inside computers may find the next section useful. Those who are not interested in such matters should turn to page 24.

BINARY ARITHMETIC AND COMPUTERS

Computers can only really deal with two numbers, one and zero. This is because computers are collections of switches. The collections are very large and the arrangements of the switches are very cunning but they remain little more than switches. Switches can be either on or off. If a switch is on this can represent all sorts of things such as " true " or " yes ". A switch in the off position will represent " false " or " no ". As far as numbers go, switches usually represent the two numbers, zero and one. If the switches can be only on or off then no other numbers can be represented. There is, however, a way of representing all the other numbers using more than one switch as a series of zeros and ones. The system which represents a quantity by a series of zeros and ones is called the " binary system ". This sounds very technical and it can be a little awkward to use until you stop trying to think in the decimal system while handling binary numbers but it is really a much simpler system of numbers than the one we are used to. With only two numbers to worry about, what else could it be but simple.

In the denary system (our normal one based on ten) there are ten digits but there is no single symbol for ten.

0 1 2 3 4 5 6 7 8 9

To represent ten we have to use two of the earlier symbols; the "0" and the "1", and put them together to make " 10 ".

The denary system is based on " powers " of ten such as 10×10 (10^2), $10 \times 10 \times 10$ (10^3) and $10 \times 10 \times 10 \times 10$ (10^4) Other, less familiar powers of ten are 10^1 and 10^0 which give ten and one. The way our numbers are written indicate how many of these powers of ten there are in the number.

Here is the way the number 2114 is interpreted in the denary system:

Column Name	Thousands	Hundreds	Tens	Units
Power of Ten	10^3	10^2	10^1	10^0
Symbol Used	2	1	1	4

Which means: 2 (lots of one thousand) plus 1 (lot of one hundred) plus 1 (lot of ten) plus 4 (lots of one)

It seems a little awkward reading a number this way but this is what we do automatically every time we read a number.

The binary system works in exactly the same way making use of powers of two rather than powers of ten. We could not write the number "2114" if we were using the binary system because there is no meaning for the symbols "2" and "4" in this system, we are restricted to the use of zeros and ones. The number 10011 in binary means:

Power of Two	2^4	2^3	2^2	2^1	2^0
Denary Equivalent	16	8	4	2	1
Symbol Used	1	0	0	1	1

Which means: 1 (lot of 16) plus 0 (lots of 8) plus 0 (lots of 4) plus 1 (lot of 2) plus 1 (lot of 1)

This adds up to the value " 19 " in the denary system.

The binary system is difficult to work with because there are a lot of separate symbols in the numbers and the symbols are very easy to get the wrong way round. "1100011001110" and "1100111001110" look almost identical yet they differ by 256 in denary.

Each of these binary digits is known as a BIT (Binary digIT). Each switch in the computer can hold one bit by being switched on or off. The switches are usually grouped in eights and a group like this is known as a BYTE. The sixteen lots of 1024 bytes of memory in the fully expanded ZX81 contains:

16 X (1024 × 8) or 1 310 072 of these switches.

These make up only the " random access memory ", there are many more of these switches in the other parts of the computer. Why 1024 though? why not 1000, a nice round number? The answer to this question is linked with binary arithmetic. Indeed, many of the numbers which crop up over and over again in computing are linked with this system of numbers.

We normally think in our familiar denary system and think of numbers such as 100 and 1000 000 as being nice, neat numbers because they are exact powers of ten. In the binary system used by computers, nice, neat numbers are exact powers of two and not ten. 1024 happens to be two, raised to the power of ten, 256 is two, raised to the power of eight. To a computer 1024 is the nice, neat number not 1000. 1K of memory contains, therefore, 1024 bytes not 1000.

The reason that an eight bit byte can store no more than 255 is that if all the eight switches were to be switched on then the number represented would be:

Bit No.	8	7	6	5	4	3	2	1
Power of Two	2^7	2^6	2^5	2^4	2^3	2^2	2^1	2^0
Value	128 +	64 +	32 +	16 +	8 +	4 +	2 +	1

which all adds up to the value 255 in denary. Adding a one to this value would result in a " carry " just as adding 1 to 9999 generates a carry.

```
 11111111          and 9999
       + 1              + 1
 ---------          -------
 100000000          10000
```

In both cases the carry means that there is an extra digit in the result. An eight bit byte can hold only eight bits, the extra one is called an overflow.

Using two bytes per number, we could hold 65 536 if all the switches were set in the on position:

1st byte 1111 1111 2nd byte 1111 1111

but the sixteenth digit has a special purpose, to represent plus or minus. Only seven of the digits can be used to represent the number and so only 32 767 can be stored. This looks like a serious reduction but there is no loss using this system. Before the range of numbers stored was from zero to 65 536 and using the 8th bit of byte two for the sign the range becomes -32 767 through zero to +32 767.

64K has a familiar ring to it as well. This is the maximum number of addresses that the Z80 central processor chip can talk to. 65 536 is another nice, neat number in the binary system, it is two raised to the power of sixteen. 256 crops up over and over again. The ZX81 has a character set with 255 codes in it. These range from 0 to 255 giving 256 numbers in all, another nice round figure in binary. 256 is two, raised to the power of eight. Keeping the number of codes to 255 means that they can all be stored in a single byte. A character string can have a maximum of 256 characters for related reasons.

CHECKING THE COSTS

The ZX81 commands, functions etc., have been investigated to find out how much memory is needed for each. The results have been organised into two reports to help you plan your programming for minimum memory usage. The first report is arranged in ascending order of memory cost and the second is arranged in alphabetical order and is much less detailed than the first. The second report acts as an index to the first. A pair of program lines have been used to find the cost of the lines being investigated:

```
1      GO TO 100
100    PRINT PEEK ( 16396 ) + PEEK ( 16397 ) * 256 - 16590 ;
" * BYTES"
```

If this program is run the result is a message " Ø BYTES " printed on the screen. If any other lines are added to the program the message will be the number of bytes of memory being used to store the extra lines. The program works by finding the address of the start of the display file in the memory. The display file is stored just above the program lines and the program lines start at 16 509. The two line program itself occupies 81 bytes and so, if (16 509 + 81) is subtracted from the byte number of the start of the display file then the result is the net cost of the lines under test. The line which sends the machine to line 100 is needed because some of the lines to be tested need variables to be set and this is not necessary if the lines being tested are by-passed. The cost is the same if the lines are met by the computer during the program or not. You may find line 100 useful as a means of keeping an eye on the amount of memory you are using as you write programs. Give it a line number which is higher than you expect to reach in the program and a GO TO command will give details of the memory used at any time. This line does not calculate the amount of memory set aside by DIM statements because this memory is assigned in the variables store which is much further on in the memory map.

It is particularly important to keep an eye on the amount of memory used by programs being written for the 1K ZX81 because of the small amount of memory available to the user. The programs in this book are mainly intended for users who have the 16K RAM pack. The jobs being tackled are much larger than the basic machine could hope to do. Most of the programs will fit into the 16K pack with lots of room to spare so why this concern with saving memory? The main reason is connected with the way that the ZX81 SAVEs and LOADs programs on cassettes. The information is transferred at a rate of about 250 bits per second. The full RAM pack will contain 16 × 1024 bytes of information and each byte is made up of 8 bits. These 131 072 bits will be transferred from the machine to the tape in about eight and a half minutes. If the program has to be both loaded and then saved each time the program is used then the transfer time will be over a quarter of an hour. The cheaper the programs are in memory, the quicker it will be to get them to and from the tape. This, and not the small size of the memory, is the most important reason for keeping things short. When your program is written and ready for use, don't forget to delete the memory checking line or strange messages will appear on the machine which will confuse any user of the program but yourself.

ZX81 MEMORY COSTS

1 BYTE

All characters entered from the keyboard when used inside strings. All single key-stroke words and symbols no matter how many characters they contain, as long as they are enclosed by quotes.

Brackets and the mathematical symbols such as " * " , " + " , " / " and " ** " all cost 1 byte. All punctuation marks cost 1 byte but the comma, when used as a print spacer, costs 15 bytes of screen memory in the display file.

NOT, used in a conditional statement costs 1 byte.

6 BYTES

All these program lines cost 6 bytes each:

10 CLS	10 CLEAR
10 CONT	10 COPY
10 FAST	10 SLOW
10 LLIST	10 LIST
10 LPRINT	10 PRINT
10 REM	10 RAND
10 RETURN	10 SCROLL
10 STOP	

7 BYTES

These are mainly versions of the 6 byte lines which can appear with extra characters. The line which prints PI is interesting because it shows that this function which is displayed as a two character symbol, only occupies 1 byte of program.

10 INPUT A	10 REM A
10 PRINT A	10 LPRINT A
10 PRINT PI	10 PRINT RND

This last line is more usually used with other functions and is dealt with more fully in the section dealing with 18 bytes.

```
10    NEXT J
```

This line is sometimes used several times in a FOR/NEXT loop and its cost as a separate line is important.

8 BYTES

10 PRINT A$	10 INPUT A$
10 PRINT ""	STEP 2 (see 23 bytes for details)
10 PRINT CHR$ A	10 PRINT STR$ A (see 14 bytes)

By subtracting the cost of 10 PRINT A from this last line we arrive at a cost of 1 byte for the additional function " CHR$ "

9 BYTES

10 PRINT LEN A$ 10 PRINT VAL A$

10 LPRINT " A " 10 PRINT CODE A$

10 LET A = B STEP -2 (see 23 bytes for details)

From this it can be seen that LEN, VAL, CODE cost 1 byte each.

10 PRINT " * " (a space) 10 PRINT " A "

Also the second half of multi-dimensional DIM statements cost 9 bytes. See 16 bytes for details.

10 BYTES

10 LET A$ = INKEY$

AND B = 1
OR B >= 1 } as part of an " IF/THEN " line, see 24 bytes

PRINT TO as part of a string slicing line, see end of this report

11 BYTES

10 LET A$ = "" (the empty string) 10 PRINT " A " ;

This makes the cost of the " ; ", 1 byte.

12 BYTES

10 LET A$ = " A " TAB (see 20 bytes for details)

13 BYTES

10 PAUSE 1 but, 10 PAUSE 10 costs 14 bytes

10 PAUSE 100 costs 15 bytes

10 PAUSE 1000 costs 16 bytes

10 GO TO 1 but, 10 GO TO 10 costs 14

10 GO TO 100 costs 15

10 GO SUB 1 but, 10 GO SUB 10 costs 14

10 GO SUB 100 costs 15

14 BYTES

```
10    PRINT STR$ 1
```

At this point it is important to point out an interesting and important fact. The ZX81 will allow the use of variable names in program lines where other computers insist on being fed the value. ZX81 users can say GO TO A or GO SUB X and, as long as the computer already knows the value of A or X then these commands will be obeyed. Under the heading " 8 Bytes " is an entry similar to the one above. The difference is that the cheaper line contains a variable name and not a number. The saving in memory is six bytes in fourteen, 43%. This is a very valuable facility indeed and its use will be seen to be of benefit in many different circumstances as more memory costs are investigated.

15 BYTES

```
10    LET A = 1          but, 10    LET A = 10 costs 16
                              10    LET A = 100 costs 17
                              10    LET A = 1.1 costs 17
10    LET A = B costs a mere 9 bytes.
```

The benefit of using variable names rather than numbers is 40% here.

The comma, when used to space out print statements costs 15 bytes of display file memory. See also 1 byte.

16 BYTES

```
10    LET A = SIN 1
```

The cost is the same for: COS, TAN, ASIN, ACOS, ATAN, INT, SGN, ABS, SQR, LN and EXP. Using the name of the variable reduces costs again.

```
10    LET A = SIN A    costs 10 bytes
10    DIM A ( 1 )    costs 16 bytes but,
10    DIM A ( 10 )   costs 17
10    DIM A ( 100 ) costs 18
10    DIM A ( 1 , 1 ) costs 24 bytes and so the "    , 1 "
```

must cost 8 bytes.

Compare this with the following:

```
10   DIM ( A )        10 bytes
10   DIM ( A , B )    12 bytes
```

When writing programs with arrays, the memory counting line will not take into consideration the space set aside in the variables store for the array elements. Allow five bytes per number in single dimensional arrays. In multi-dimensional arrays multiply together the numbers inside the brackets and then multiply the result by five. The result is the number of bytes set aside in the variables store for the array.

```
10   DIM A ( 5 , 10 ) sets aside 250 bytes for array A.
10   PRINT PEEK ( 1 ) but, 10 PRINT PEEK ( 10 ) costs
                                                17 bytes
                          10 PRINT PEEK ( 100 ) costs 18
```

The more usual address size to be found in a PEEK line such as this is:

```
10   PRINT PEEK ( 10 000 ) and the cost of this is 20 bytes.
```

17 BYTES

```
10   DIM A$ ( 1 ) costs one byte more than
10   DIM A ( 1 )
```

so all the string array dimensioning lines will cost a byte more than the corresponding number array line. There is an important difference between the two types of arrays, string arrays only occupy one byte per character and not five.

```
10 DIM A$ ( 5 , 10 ) sets aside only 50 bytes.
```

18 BYTES

```
10   PRINT INT (RND * 9 )
```

The use of the RND function has been looked at earlier under 7 bytes but this is the more usual form of a line using this function. The variation using the variable name saves memory again

```
10   PRINT INT ( RND X ) costs only 12 bytes.
```

10 PRINT TAB 1 ; " A "

but TAB costs vary with the different print positions. The cost is incurred in the display file and not in the area of memory where the program lines are stored.

10 PRINT TAB X ; " A " costs a mere 12 bytes.

As the cost of:

10 PRINT " A " is 9 bytes, the " TAB X ; " bit can only cost 3 bytes.

19 BYTES

Subroutines cost a minimum of 19 bytes.

```
1   GO TO 9   costs 13 bytes  )
9   GO SUB 5                  ) Costs 32 bytes so the
5   RETURN                    ) subroutine costs 19
```

When subroutines are used it is always necessary to by-pass them and a GO TO line is necessary. If, however, the subroutines are all grouped together then the one GO TO line will serve for all the routines.

21 BYTES

```
10  POKE 1 , 1          but, 10  POKE 10 , 1 costs 22 bytes
                             10  POKE 10 000 , 1 costs 25
                             10  POKE 10 000 , 10 costs 26
10  POKE A , A costs 9 bytes
10  PLOT 1 , 1          but, 10  PLOT 1 , 10 costs 22 bytes
                             10  PLOT 1 , 40 costs 23 bytes
10  PLOT A , A costs 9 bytes
```

All the UNPLOT commands have the same costs. The cost of the plot position which is incurred in the display file is one byte per print position and therefore, one byte per two plot positions.

23 BYTES

10 LET A = 2 * 2 costs 23 bytes but as;

10 LET A = 2 costs 15

the cost of the number and the multiplication sign is 8 bytes. The alternative method of calculating a square costs the same amount of memory:

10 LET A = 2 ** 2

10 LET A = -2 * -2 costs 25 bytes and

10 LET A = -2 ** 2 is cheaper at 24 bytes but gives the wrong answer!

All squared numbers are positive and the ZX81 gives a negative answer. This means that there is a bug in the language. If you are writing programs with squares to be calculated it will be necessary to include an ABS in every line which includes the function, " ** ".

10 FOR J = 1 TO 9 costs 23 bytes but,

10 FOR J = 1 TO 10 costs 24

10 FOR J = 1 TO 9 STEP 2 costs 31 bytes so the

" STEP 2 " bit must cost 8

The basic cost of a FOR/NEXT loop is:

10 FOR J = 1 TO 9
20 NEXT J } 30 bytes

24 BYTES

10 IF A = 1 THEN GO TO 9 but,

10 IF A = 1 THEN GO TO 10 costs 25

The use of " <= ", " < ", " > " and " <> " in lines like this all give identical costs.

10 IF A = 1 OR B < 2 THEN GO TO 9 costs 34 bytes so the

" OR B < 2 " costs 10

10 IF NOT A = 1 THEN GO TO 9 costs 25 bytes so the

NOT must be only 1 byte.

10 IF A = 1 THEN GO SUB 9 also costs 24 bytes

but there will have to be at least one extra GO TO line to by-pass this subroutine. If all the subroutines are at the end of the program then a STOP line would be cheaper at only 6 bytes.

The ZX81 will accept variable names in GO TO and GO SUB instructions and so savings are to be had here as well.

PRINTING WITH AND WITHOUT FRILLS

PRINT AT

10 PRINT " A " costs a basic 9 bytes

10 PRINT AT 1 , 1 ; " A " costs 26 so the

" AT 1 , 1 ; " bit costs 17

most of which is for the two numbers.

10 PRINT AT L , L ; " A " costs only 14 bytes

Each print position along the line will cost an extra byte in the display file.

TAB

10 PRINT TAB 1 ; " A " costs 18 bytes which makes the cost of the " TAB 1 ; " part of the line 9 bytes.

10 PRINT TAB X ; " A " costs only 12 bytes of program space.

COMPARING PRINT AT WITH THE USE OF EMPTY PRINT STATEMENTS

10 PRINT AT 4 , 1 ; " A " costs 26 bytes but,

```
10  PRINT
11  PRINT
12  PRINT          } costs 27 bytes
13  PRINT " A "
```

So it is well worth using empty print statements to space out text by one or two blank lines. To leave three or more lines unprinted, it is cheaper to use the "print at" statement. To print in from the left hand margin a TAB statement will have to be built into the last print line. This will raise the cost by ten bytes and cut down the number of empty print lines which can be used and still show a saving.

```
10   PRINT                  }
11   PRINT TAB 5 ; " A "    }  costs 24 bytes
```

while:

```
10   PRINT AT 2 , 5 ; " A " costs 26 bytes
```

The extra effort might not be thought to be worth the two byte saving.

If variable names can be used instead of numbers then "Printing With Frills" can be as cheap as it is effective and convenient

```
10   PRINT AT X , Y ; " A " costs only 14 bytes to store in
```

the program area.

STRING SLICING

```
10   PRINT A$ costs a basic 8 bytes
10   PRINT A$ ( TO 9 ) costs 18 bytes so the
" ( TO 9 ) " costs 10 bytes
10   PRINT A$ ( TO 10 ) costs 19 because of the extra
                                    character
10   PRINT A$ ( 1 TO 9 ) costs 25 bytes.
```

The " (1 TO 9) " costs 17 bytes

The last alternative:

```
10   PRINT A$ ( 1 TO ) costs 18 bytes as might have been
                                    expected.
```

Here again, considerable savings are to be made by the use of variable names in the place of numbers.

```
10   PRINT A$ ( A TO B ) costs 13 bytes
```

compared with the 25 for the line which uses the values directly.

MEMORY COST INDEX

SAVING TIME

The first draft of the word processing program described in a later chapter had more or less the same number of lines of code as the final version. The problem with the first program was that it was too slow and the machine would not accept characters at anything like normal typing speed. The rate at which the computer would accept key-strokes was considerably increased by the simple expedient of re-locating some of the lines. The bulk of a word processor's time is spent in writing and remembering text. This text will need editing and so it is vitally important that the computer is able to break off from this job to move the cursor round in the text and prepare for corrections and additions. The signal which tells the ZX81 to stop writing the next few key-strokes onto the screen and treat them as cursor control signals is the entry of a " > ". The first draft had a loop which included lines something like these:

```
10      INPUT A$
20      IF A$ = " > " THEN INPUT B$
30      IF A$ = " > " AND B$ = " 6 " THEN LET L = L + 1
40      IF A$ = " > " AND B$ = " 6 " THEN SCROLL
50      IF A$ = " > " AND B$ = " 8 " THEN LET C = C + 1
60      IF A$ = " > " AND B$ = " 5 " THEN LET C = C - 1
70      IF A$ = " > " AND B$ = " 7 " THEN LET P = P - 2
80      IF A$ = " > " AND B$ = " 7 " THEN GO SUB 930
```

and several more similar lines before the few lines which did most of the work. These lines were only concerned with the editing side of the job and were used only infrequently but it was having to read all these that slowed up the machine so much. These seldom used lines were moved out of the loop and all that was necessary was to include this line:

```
20      IF A$ = " > " THEN GO TO (the section of the
program which dealt with the cursor control)
```

If you decide to use the word processing package you will find that, while not as fast as an electric typewriter, it will accept a regular, rhythmic style of typing at quite a reasonable rate.

Speeding-up techniques fall into two main groups; keeping loops tidy and being careful about the choice of mathematical function in number work. This next example of a method of saving processing time is a hybrid of the two. In some mathematical programs the same operation is performed many times and the use of loops is essential. If it were necessary to construct a table of $J^2 \div \sqrt{K}$ for values of J = 1 to 10 and values of K = 1 to 100 then the following lines might be used:

```
FOR J = 1 TO 10
FOR K = 1 TO 100
LET A = J ** 2 / SQR K
NEXT K
NEXT J
```

Processing time 3 min. 48 sec.

(FAST mode)

```
FOR J = 1 TO 10
LET B = J ** 2
FOR K = 1 TO 100
LET A = B / SQR K
NEXT K
NEXT J
```

Processing time 2 min. 1 sec.

(FAST mode)

In the first version, the square of J had to be calculated 1000 times but this slow calculation was needed only 10 times in the second version of the program. This pair of programs shows how important it is to be careful in the structuring of loops but also how slow the ZX81 is at finding squares and square roots. There is no easy alternative to the use of the SQR function but there are alternative ways of finding squares and other powers of numbers. The square of two can be generated in the following ways:

2 + 2 = 4　　　2 * 2 = 4　　　2 ** 2 = 4

and it might be interesting to find out how quickly the machine finds the square by these three methods.

```
FOR J = 1 TO 1000
LET A = 2 ** 2
NEXT J
PRINT " DONE "
```

1 min. 56 sec.

```
FOR J = 1 TO 1000
LET A = 2 * 2
NEXT J
PRINT " DONE "
```

8 sec.

```
FOR J = 1 TO 1000
LET A = 2 + 2
NEXT J
PRINT " DONE "
```

7 sec.

There is not much to be gained by replacing multiplication with multiple addition but a lot of time to be saved by replacing the " raised to the power of " function with multiple multiplication. In a loop like the one above this line:

```
LET A   2 * 2 * 2 * 2 * 2 * 2 * 2 * 2 * 2 * 2
```

took only 24 seconds to work out a thousand times. Having started to look at the time taken to run programs it might be as well to check that memory saving does not push up the time taken to process information. The one message that emerged from the investigation of memory cost was that the use of variable names was to be much preferred. Does the adoption of this technique slow down processing? After all the machine has to look up the value of the variable each time.

10 FOR J = 1 TO 1000	10 LET B = 10
20 LET A = 10	20 FOR J = 1 TO 1000
30 NEXT J	30 LET A = B
40 PRINT " DONE "	40 NEXT J
	50 PRINT " DONE "
1 min. 7 sec. (SLOW mode)	1 min. 0 sec. (SLOW mode)

Not only does this technique save memory and therefore save on SAVE and LOAD time but it also saves a little processing time as well.

On some computers it is worthwhile putting all the subroutines at the start of the program listing if the routines are called repeatedly. This is because the machine starts looking for the line specified in the GO SUB instruction at line 1 and routines stored at the top of the program are found faster than those stored at the end. The ZX81 is different. To GO SUB 5000 a thousand times takes slightly less time than to GO SUB 5. Having the subroutines at the start does, however, have an advantage. The program lines which call the routine have less characters in them e.g.

GO SUB 5 compared with GO SUB 5000

This is a small saving but many such savings can add up to a significant amount.

Having worked back to saving bytes again there are a few more ways of keeping memory use to a minimum before we are done. The first is simplicity itself but often overlooked.

```
10      LET A = 2
20      LET B = A ** 2
30      PRINT B
```

costs 39 memory bytes whereas;

```
10      LET A = 2
20      PRINT A ** 2
```

costs only 30

There is no need to store the calculated value before printing it unless it is needed in further calculation.

If you are feeling really miserly about the use of memory, consider the use of single key-stroke words in PRINT statements. It is possible to print such useful words as " RETURN ", " INPUT ", " THEN " and " STOP " with a convenient space fore and aft, all for the cost of a single byte. Put the required word on the screen with the computer in command mode (with the K cursor) and then enclose it with inverted commas and build up the rest of the print statement around it. It is a bit of a chore but you do save a lot of memory.

Here is another, slightly more realistic, method of saving memory when printing material. Say, for reasons best known to yourself, you want to print " THE QUICK RED FOX JUMPED OVER THE LAZY BROWN DOG ". Keying this in as a line:

```
10      PRINT " THE QUICK RED ..... etc.
```

costs 56 bytes and prints rather badly. Line one finishes with " TH " and the next line starts with " E LAZY ... ". The most usual answer to this problem is to write two lines:

```
10      PRINT " THE QUICK RED FOX JUMPED OVER "
20      PRINT " THE LAZY BROWN DOG "
```

but the cost immediately rises to 63 bytes. It is cheaper to use up to six spaces to pad out the text and make it fit than it is to write a new line. The ZX81 will take very long lines of text compared with most computers.

The most effective way of saving memory on print statements is to be really mean with the characters. This mean streak has to become a habit if you are to keep the cost of your programs consistently low. You may have noticed the use of the word "KEY" in the programs in this book in place of the more usual "ENTER". This simple habit costs no effort and saves two bytes each time it is used.

SUMMARY

The chapter started with a comparison of the ZX81 with its predecessor, the ZX80. The different methods of storing numbers was looked at in some detail and was seen to be the reason for the big difference in processing speeds. This section was developed into an account of computer arithmetic based on the binary system for interested readers.

The much lower processing speed of the ZX81 and its less efficient use of memory led into a discussion of the cost of the functions available on the new machine.

A means of checking the memory being used by programs was discussed in detail and this method was used to calculate the cost of each function. Techniques for improving processing speeds were looked at and a number of useful methods were identified.

The main memory saving technique which emerged was the use of variable names in place of numbers in the program lines. Less spectacular methods were introduced and the development of these into programming habits was recommended.

It was noted that the saving of memory was less important than the consequent saving of program LOAD and SAVE time. This is because of the rather slow speed of data transfer via the cassette interface.

4 Word Juggler

A convenient instruction table for using WORD JUGGLER can be found on page 161.

WORD PROCESSING AND READING AGE

YOU WILL HAVE NOTICED THE SUDDEN CHANGE IN STYLE OF PRESENTATION. THE MAXIMUM OF THIRTY-TWO CHARACTERS PER LINE MAY HAVE GIVEN THE GAME AWAY ALREADY - OR MAYBE THE TYPE FACE HAS A FAMILIAR LOOK. BUT WHATEVER THE REASON, YOU WILL HAVE GUESSED CORRECTLY THAT THIS CHAPTER HAS BEEN SET USING THE ZX81 AS A WORD PROCESSOR. PROCESSOR IS A BIT TOO TECHNICAL A TITLE FOR THE PROGRAM, IT IS CALLED *WORD JUGGLER*. SETTING A CHAPTER IN THIS WAY SEEMED A GOOD WAY TO SHOW THE PROGRAM OFF.

AS WELL AS WORD PROCESSING, THIS CHAPTER DEALS WITH AN ADD-ON FACILITY TO BE USED WITH THE PROCESSOR, A READING AGE CALCULATOR. MANY OF THE USES OF THE ZX81 CENTRE AROUND EDUCATION AND READERS MAY WANT TO USE A WORD PROCESSOR TO PRODUCE TEXT FOR THEIR STUDENTS. IN THE EXCITEMENT OF THE CREATIVE MOMENT IT IS ALL TOO EASY TO WRITE MATERIAL WHICH IS TOO DIFFICULT. WORDS WHICH

FOOTNOTE

Because, at the time of going to press, the ZX printer was still not fully developed, the material presented here is a simulation of the printer's output using an IBM printer.

ARE VERY EFFICIENT AT CONVEYING INFORMATION BUT TOO HARD FOR THE LESS ABLE READER MAY SLIP INTO THE TEXT. SENTENCES MAY BECOME TOO LONG FOR THE YOUNG MIND TO HOLD ALL AT ONCE. THE READING AGE OF THE TEXT MAY RISE ABOVE THE AGE OF THE READERS.

AN ADD-ON SEGMENT OF THE PROGRAM WILL ENABLE THE AUTHOR TO KEEP AN EYE ON THE DEMANDS THE TEXT WILL MAKE ON THE READERS. THE READING AGE IS CALCULATED AFTER EACH PARAGRAPH AND IS DISPLAYED AT THE BOTTOM OF THE SCREEN TOGETHER WITH THE CURRENT PARAGRAPH NUMBER. NOT ALL USERS WILL NEED THIS FACILITY SO THE FEW LINES OF PROGRAM WHICH MAKE IT AVAILABLE ARE GIVEN AT THE END OF THE LISTING. THIS MEANS THAT THERE WILL BE GAPS IN THE LINE NUMBERS SO DONT WORRY, ALL THE NECESSARY LINES ARE THERE.

WHAT IS THE WORD JUGGLER GOING TO BE ABLE TO DO? WELL, PERSONALISED, RIGHT HAND MARGIN JUSTIFIED LETTERS TO ALL THE PEOPLE ON A MAILING LIST IS A LITTLE BEYOND THE CAPABILITIES BUT THE LIST ITSELF IS PERFECTLY POSSIBLE. INSERTING A LENGTHY SECTION INTO A FINISHED PIECE IS A LITTLE TOO MUCH TO EXPECT BUT CORRECTIONS, RESTRUCTURING OF A SENTENCE AND SMALL ADDITIONS ARE NOT. THE MACHINE WILL COPE WITH LARGER JOBS BUT TAKES SO LONG TO DO THEM IN BASIC THAT THEY HAVE BEEN SHELVED FOR NOW. THESE FACILITIES WILL HAVE TO WAIT FOR A ZX81 MACHINE CODE PROGRAMMING

BOOK AT PRESENT IN THE PLANNING STAGE.

THE PROGRAM DESCRIBED HERE WILL ALLOW THE TYPING OF TEXT INTO THE COMPUTER WITHOUT THE USE OF COMMANDS OR THE NEWLINE KEY (UP-GRADED ZX80 USERS WILL HAVE TO USE NEWLINE OR TYPE BLIND). AS THE TEXT IS STORED IN THE PROG-RAM AND NOT IN VARIABLES, IT IS NOT LOST IF *RUN* OR *CLEAR* ARE USED BY MISTAKE. AS WELL AS ALT-ERATIONS, WHOLE PARAGRAPHS CAN BE DELETED QUICKLY AND EASILY. THE MATERIAL CAN BE RUN THROUGH FOR READING AND THE PRINT OR AM-END POSITION IS EASILY SET ANY-WHERE IN THE TEXT BY USING THE CURSOR CONTROL KEYS. THESE KEYS GIVE COARSE AS WELL AS FINE CON-TROL.

HOW IS THE JUGGLER TO BE USED? THE POSSIBILITY OF USING IT TO RUN A MAILING LIST HAS BEEN MEN-TIONED, HERE ARE A FEW MORE POSS IBILITIES. READERS WILL PROBAB-LY DEVISE MANY OTHERS.

1) THE SCREEN MAY BE USED AS THE PRESENTATION MEDIUM. LARGE CHUNKS OF INFORMATION CAN BE MADE TO ROLL UP THE SCREEN AT THE USERS COMMAND OR UNDER AUTOMATIC CONTROL. THIS MAY BE USEFUL FOR THE PHYSICALLY HANDICAPPED. ROUGHLY TEN BOOK PAGES CAN BE READ BEFORE HELP IS NEEDED.

2) CLUBS OR SMALL BUSINESSES MAY FIND A LIST OF MEMBERS OR CUS TOMERS USEFUL. COMPANY REPS CALLING SCHEDULES CAN BE SET

UP AND MAINTAINED IN THE SAME WAY.

3) IN SOME GAMES PROGRAMS A LOT OF INSTRUCTION HAS TO BE SET OUT FOR NEW PLAYERS. THE WORD JUGGLER MAKES THE ENTRY OF SUCH INFORMATION EASY AND ENSURES THAT SCREEN PRESENTATION IS RIGHT FIRST TIME. ONCE THE TEXT IS IN, THE BULK OF THE JUGGLER CAN BE DELETED LEAVING JUST THE SECTION THAT DISPLAYS THE INSTRUCTIONS.

4) IF THE PROGRAM IS USED TO PREPARE ARTICLES AND CHAPTERS OF BOOKS THE SAVING IN CORRECTION FLUID IS ENORMOUS AND THAT EXTRA CARBON COPY WHICH WAS NEVER ANTICIPATED CAN BE QUICKLY RUN OFF.

THE PROGRAM IS REALLY QUITE SIMPLE AND NOT TOO LONG. IT MIGHT NOT SEEM VERY SIMPLE AT FIRST BECAUSE IT MAKES EXTENSIVE USE OF PEEK AND POKE. IT IS NOT THE COMMANDS THEMSELVES WHICH ARE OFF-PUTTING SO MUCH AS THE VERY LARGE NUMBERS THAT SEEM TO BE SCATTERED FREELY THROUGH PROGRAMS WHICH MAKE USE OF THESE COMMANDS. A GREAT DEAL OF CARE HAS BEEN TAKEN WITH THE DOCUMENTATION OF THE PEEK AND POKE LINES. THE NUMBERS ARE MEMORY ADDRESSES AT WHICH USEFUL INFORMATION IS STORED. THE ADDRESS IS GIVEN IN ENGLISH EACH TIME ONE COMES UP IN NUMBERS FOR EXAMPLE:

POKE 19365, PEEK (19365) + 128 MEANS LOOK AT THE NEXT CHARACTER (STORED AT 19365), ADD 128 TO IT

AND PUT THE RESULT BACK IN THE SAME STORE. ALL THE INVERSE VIDEO CHARACTERS HAVE CODES 128 MORE THAN THE NORMAL ONES. THE RESULT IS THAT AN INVERSE CURSOR IS GENERATED. A LINE LIKE THIS IS USED IN THE PROGRAM.

THE TEXT IS STORED IN STRINGS AND THIS MIGHT SEEM TO LIMIT THE AMOUNT OF STORAGE. THERE ARE 26 STRINGS, A$ TO Z$ AND EACH CAN HOLD 256 CHARACTERS. THIS ADDS UP TO ONLY 6656 LETTERS AND SPACES, MUCH LESS THAN THE ZX81 CAN HOLD. MORE OF THE SPACE CAN BE OCCUPIED IF ONLY ONE STRING, A$, IS USED. THIS SOUNDS MOST UNLIKELY BUT THIS IS HOW IT IS DONE. STARTING AT LINE 100 IS A SERIES OF 2 LINE SUB-ROUTINES LIKE THIS ONE:

```
100 LET A$=     192 SPACES
101 RETURN
```

192 SPACES IS 6 LINES OF SCREEN SPACE AND THIS WILL BE KNOWN AS A *PARAGRAPH*. 3 OF THESE PARAGRAPHS ARE PRINTED AT A TIME BY MEANS OF LINES WHICH SAY:

```
GO SUB 100   PRINT A$
GO SUB 102   PRINT A$
GO SUB 104   PRINT A$.
```

AT FIRST, CHARACTERS ARE POKED INTO THESE EMPTY STRINGS. LATER THE CONTENTS OF THE STRINGS CAN BE RE-PRINTED FOR CHECKING AND EDITING. STICKING TO A$ MEANS THAT ONLY ONE STRING WILL CLUTTER UP THE SEPARATE AREA OF MEMORY WHERE THE VARIABLES ARE HELD.

TO HELP THE RUNNING OF THE PROGRAM ALL THE LINES WHICH HOLD THE TEXT MUST HAVE THE SAME NUMBER OF DIGITS IN THEIR NUMBERS. THE SPACE BETWEEN LINES 100 AND 999 WILL HOLD 449 OF THESE SUBROUTINES. THIS IS MORE THAN ENOUGH TO EXPLOIT ALL THE SPACE THAT THE EXPANDED ZX81 CAN OFFER.

THE PROGRAM ITSELF TAKES 3.5K OF MEMORY SO ONLY 12.5 ARE AVAILABLE FOR TEXT STORAGE. 57 OF THE 6 LINE PARAGRAPHS CAN BE HELD IN THE COMPUTER BEFORE MEMORY LIMITATIONS CAUSE TROUBLE. THIS IS EQUIVALENT TO AROUND 2000 WORDS, A GOOD SIZED ESSAY.

SETTING UP THE STORAGE SPACE
THERE IS NO GETTING AWAY FROM THE FACT THAT YOU ARE GOING TO HAVE TO KEY IN 192 SPACES BUT, DONT WORRY, YOU WILL ONLY HAVE TO DO IT ONCE. THE OTHER 56 PARAGRAPHS CAN ALL BE SET UP USING THE EDIT KEY. KEY IN THESE LINES

```
1    GO TO 3000
100  LET A$= " (192 SPACES)"
101  PRINT LEN A$
```

AND RUN THE PROGRAM TO MAKE SURE THAT THE STRING IS EXACTLY 192 SPACES LONG. NEXT REPLACE LINE 101 WITH:

```
101 RETURN
```

NOW THAT ONE OF THE SUB-ROUTINES IS SET UP CORRECTLY IT CAN BE USED AS THE MODEL FOR ALL THE OTHERS. USE THE CURSOR CONTROL KEY (SHIFT 7) TO SET THE CURRENT LINE TO 100. USE (SHIFT 0) TO RUB OUT THE LINE NUMBER AND THEN GIVE THE LINE THE NEW NUMBER OF

102. SIMPLY KEY NEW LINE TO ENTER PARAGRAPH TWO AT A COST OF MUCH LESS EFFORT THAN THE FIRST ONE. REPEAT THIS PROCESS UNTIL FIVE PARAGRAPHS HAVE BEEN SET UP. THIS WILL BE ENOUGH FOR TEST PURPOSES AND THE SAVE/LOAD TIME WILL BE KEPT TO A REASONABLE LENGTH. THE BULK OF THE SPACE CAN BE SET UP IN THE SAME WAY WHEN THE PROGRAM IS RUNNING SMOOTHLY. DONT FORGET TO KEY IN THE RETURN LINES TO FINISH OFF THE SUBROUTINES. ALL THESE WILL HAVE ODD NUMBERS.

THE SPACE ABOVE LINE 220 CAN BE USED FOR THE MAIN PROGRAM BUT THE LINES BETWEEN 1 AND 100 MUST BE LEFT STRICTLY ALONE. THE PROGRAM ONLY WORKS BECAUSE THE ZX81 KNOWS EXACTLY WHICH MEMORY STORE HOLDS THE FIRST CHARACTER IN THE FIRST STRING. ONE CHARACTER BETWEEN LINE 1 AND 100 AND THE MACHINE WILL NO LONGER KNOW WHERE IT IS AND THE PROGRAM WILL CRASH. NOW THAT WE HAVE OUR STORAGE SET UP HOW DO WE START USING IT? THE SCREEN IS THE FIRST DESTINATION OF THE TEXT. ONCE THERE IT CAN BE CHANGED, ADDED TO OR DELETED UNTIL THE WRITER IS SATISFIED WITH THE PRODUCT. THE TEXT IS ENTERED, ONE CHARACTER AT A TIME AND POKED ONTO LINE 7 OF THE SCREEN. WHEN LINE 7 IS FULL ITS CONTENTS ARE POKED INTO THE PROGRAM, LINE 7 IS SCROLLED TO BECOME LINE 6, RELEASING LINE 7 FOR THE NEXT 32 CHARACTERS. THE INVERSE VIDEO CURSOR SHOWS THE PRINT POSITION ALONG LINE 7 AT ALL TIMES. THE BIG ADVANTAGE OF

ALWAYS WORKING ON LINE SEVEN IS THAT 3 PARAGRAPHS CAN BE DISPLAYED GIVING THE CONTEXT OF THE MIDDLE ONE. THIS IS ESPECIALLY IMPORTANT WHEN THE TEXT IS BEING EDITED.

IN ORDER TO LIFT CHARACTERS FROM THE SCREEN FOR PERMANENT STORAGE IN THE STRINGS IT IS IMPORTANT TO KNOW WHERE THE DISPLAY FILE IS STORED IN THE MEMORY. IN MOST COMPUTERS, THE SCREEN FILE IS IN A SECTION OF MEMORY WHICH IS PER MANENTLY SET ASIDE FOR THAT PURPOSE. SETTING ASIDE 704 BYTES NECESSARY TO HOLD THE SCREEN ON THE BASIC ZX81 WOULD USE SO MUCH OF THE SMALL MEMORY THAT NO SPACE WOULD BE LEFT FOR ANY PROGRAM SO ONLY THE MINIMUM SPACE IS USED. A CONSEQUENCE OF THIS IS THAT THE DISPLAY FILE MOVES ABOUT IN THE MEMORY AND HAS TO BE FOUND. FORTUNATELY, ALL THAT IS NECESSARY IS TO ASK THE COMPUTER WHERE IT IS. THE INFORMATION IS STORED IN A PAIR OF BYTES WHICH HAVE THE ADDRESSES 16396 AND 16397. THE ADDRESS OF THE FIRST BYTE OF THE SCREEN FILE IS DIVIDED BY 256 AND STORED IN THE SECOND OF THESE BYTES. ANY REMAINDER IS STORED IN THE FIRST OF THE BYTES. THIS MAY SEEM VERY COMPLICATED BUT IT IS THE WAY THE COMPUTER HAS TO WORK. TO REGENERATE THE ADDRESS THE PROCESS HAS TO BE REVERSED BY MEANS OF THIS LINE:

```
LET A=PEEK (16396) +PEEK
      (16397) *256
```

THIS SETS *A* TO THE FIRST BYTE OF THE DISPLAY FILE.

ALTHOUGH THERE ARE 32 CHARACTERS TO THE LINE THE DISPLAY FILE HAS 33. THE LAST ONE IS A SPECIAL CHARACTER WHICH TELLS THE MACHINE TO START PRINTING ANOTHER LINE. THE START OF LINE 7 IS A LITTLE FURTHER ON THAN THE VALUE STORED IN *A*. IT IS, IN FACT, (6 TIMES 33) BYTES FURTHER ON.TO FIND THE MEMORY STORE IN WHICH THE FIRST CHARACTER OF LINE 7 IS STORED A LINE LIKE THIS IS USED:

```
LET A=198+PEEK (16396) +PEEK
      (16397) *256
```

BUT, BEFORE EVEN THIS WILL WORK THE SCREEN FILE MUST HAVE SOMETHING IN IT. SPACES WILL DO AND SO ALL WE NEED DO IS PRINT 3 OF THE EMPTY PARAGRAPHS BEFORE PEEKING.

HAVING FOUND THE START OF LINE 7 IT IS A SIMPLE MATTER TO KEEP TRACK OF THE NEXT POSITION ALONG THE LINE. A COUNTER, *C*, IS SET TO 1 AND THEN INCREMENTED EACH TIME A CHARACTER IS ENTERED. WHEN C=32 IT IS TIME TO STORE THAT LINE IN THE PROGRAM AND GO ON TO THE NEXT. THE LINE WHICH FINDS THE START OF LINE SEVEN IS USED OVER AND OVER AND SO IS PUT INTO A SUB-ROUTINE WHICH ORGANISES THE PRINTING. CHARACTERS ARE POKED ONTO THE SCREEN AND NOT *PRINTED* FOR SEVERAL REASONS. IF TWO CHARACTERS WERE PUT IN AT ONCE BY MISTAKE THEN THE CHARACTER COUNTING WOULD BE OUT BY ONE, THE NEWLINE CHARACTER WOULD BE OBLITERATED AND THE VIDEO WOULD CRASH. THE DISPLAY

IS SPECTACULAR WHEN THIS HAPPENS BUT THE PROGRAM CANNOT BE RESCUED. ANOTHER REASON FOR POKING IS THAT MESSAGES ARE PRINTED AT THE BOTTOM OF THE SCREEN SO THE PRINT POSITION WOULD HAVE TO BE REPEATEDLY RESET. THIS WILL NEED EXTRA CODE BUT THE PROGRAM WILL BE FAST ENOUGH ONLY IF THE NUMBER OF STATEMENTS BETWEEN EACH CHARACTER ENTRY IS KEPT TO A MIN IMUM.

THE FIRST JOB TO DO AFTER ENTERING A CHARACTER IS TO TURN THE NEXT CHARACTER ON THE SCREEN INTO AN INVERSE VIDEO VERSION OF ITSELF. HERE ARE THE ROUTINES WHICH FIND THE APPROPRIATE PARAGRAPHS, PRINT THEM AND THEN SET UP THE CURSOR.

```
900    LET A = 198 + PEEK
( 16396 ) + PEEK ( 16397 ) * 256
901    RETURN
910    CLS
911    IF P > 57 THEN GO TO 2990
912    FAST
913    GO SUB P * 2 + 98
914    PRINT A$
915    GO SUB P * 2 + 100
916    PRINT A$
917    GO SUB P * 2 + 102
918    PRINT A$
919    PRINT AT 19 , 0 ;
" PARAGRAPH * " ; P
920    SLOW
921    RETURN
```

AND NOW THE ROUTINE THAT SETS THE PARAGRAPH NUMBER AND CALLS THE PREVIOUS ROUTINE.

```
930     LET P = P + 1
931     GO SUB 910
932     GO SUB 900
933     RETURN
```

THIS ROUTINE IS CALLED WHENEVER THE COMPUTER NEEDS TO MOVE TO A DIFFERENT PARAGRAPH. IT ADDS ONE TO *P*,THE PARAGRAPH COUNTER AND THEN PRINTS THE NEW PARAGRAPH WITH THE PRECEDING AND FOLLOWING PARAGRAPHS TO GIVE CONTEXT.

SETTING UP THE FIRST SECTION
VERY FEW VARIABLES ARE USED IN THE WORD JUGGLER.WE HAVE MET *P* AND*C*. *L* KEEPS TRACK OF THE LINE NUMBER,*J* AND *K* ARE USED AS LOOP COUNTERS. IF THE READING AGE CALCULATOR IS ADDED TO THE PROGRAM THEN THE VARIABLES *LT* (NO.OF LETTERS),*ST* (NO.OF SENTENCES) AND *WD* (NO. OF WORDS) WILL BE USED. THE INKEY$ FUNCTION READS THE KEYBOARD.
EACH KEY-STROKE IS FED INTO A$ BY LINE 1100. ALL KEY STROKES WHICH WOULD GIVE MORE THAN ONE CHARACTER HAVE CODES WHICH ARE MORE THAN 63. LINE 1120 ELIMINATES ALL THESE. THE ONLY KEY THAT CAUSES TROUBLE IS THE SPACE KEY BECAUSE IT ACTS AS A *BREAK* INSTRUCTION AND STOPS THE INKEY$ CYCLE. THERE IS A SOLUTION TO THIS A LITTLE LATER ON. MEANWHILE HERE IS THE FIRST SEGMENT OF THE PROGRAM:

```
1000   LET P = 0
1030   GO SUB 930
1040   LET C = 1
1050   LET L = 1
1070   POKE A + C , PEEK
( A + C ) + 128
1080   IF INKEY$ <>" " THEN GO
TO 1080
1090   IF INKEY$ = " " THEN GO
TO 1090
1100   LET A$ = INKEY$
1110   IF A$ = " " " " THEN GO
TO 2990
1120   IF CODE ( A$ ) > 63 THEN
GO TO 1080
```

SO FAR WE KNOW WHAT HAS BEEN ENTERED AND THE DIFFICULT CHARACTERS HAVE BEEN REJECTED. (SHIFT Q) HAS BEEN USED AS A MEANS OF STOPPING THE PROCESS SO THAT THE TEXT CAN BE PRINTED OR STORED ON TAPE. WE NOW HAVE TO FIND A WAY OF PRINTING A SPACE WITHOUT STOPPING THE PROGRAM AND A WAY TO MOVE INTO *EDIT* MODE. (SHIFT M) IS USED TO SIGNAL A CHANGE TO EDIT MODE AND ZERO IS USED AS A MEANS OF PRINTING A SPACE WITHOUT USING THE BREAK KEY. WHEN WRITING TEXT ALONE, *O* CAN BE USED FOR ZERO. LINE 1140 CONVERTS A ZERO INTO A SPACE.

NO INVERTED COMMAS HAVE BEEN USED IN THIS CHAPTER, * * HAS BEEN USED INSTEAD. IF INVERTED COMMAS WERE TO BE POKED INTO A

STRING THEN THE MACHINE WOULD INTERPRET THIS AS THE END OF THE STRING AND THE STRUCTURE OF THE STORAGE WOULD BE SPOILED. SO, YOU HAVE TO AVOID:(SHIFT P), THE BREAK KEY AND ZERO (IF YOU WANT NOUGHT AND NOT A SPACE). THESE ARE FAIRLY EASY RULES TO LEARN AND SOON MASTERED. YOU WILL FIND DETAILS OF HOW TO USE THE WORD JUGGLER AT THE END OF THE CHAPTER. NEXT IS THE SECTION OF CODE WHICH DOES THE PRINTING.

```
1130   IF A$ = " > " THEN GO TO
1500
1140   IF A$ = " 0 " THEN LET
A$ = " * "
1170   POKE A + C , CODE ( A$ )
1180   LET C = C + 1
1190   IF C = 33 THEN GO TO 1300
1200   GO TO 1070
```

NOW THAT THE FIRST LINE HAS BEEN WRITTEN TO THE AUTHORS SATISFACT ION, IT CAN BE COPIED INTO THE STRINGS. 16501 HAPPENS TO BE THE ADDRESS OF THE FIRST SPACE IN THE FIRST STRING AT LINE 102. THE FIRST CHARACTER OF THE FIRST LINE HAS TO BE STORED HERE. THE EASIEST WAY TO STORE THIS CHARA- CTER AND THE OTHER 31 IN THEIR CORRECT PLACES IS TO SET UP A FOR/NEXT LOOP WHICH CYCLES 32 TIMES. THE LOOP COUNTER WILL DO A LOT OF THE WORK AND THE ONLY JOB LEFT TO DO IS TO ALLOW FOR CHANGES IN THE LINE NUMBER.

```
1340 POKE 16501+J+(L*32)+(P*209)
     , PEEK (A-33+J)  MEANS;
```

START AT 16501, ADD THE POSITION OF THE CHARACTER ALONG LINE 7, ADD 32 FOR EVERY LINE USED IN THIS PARAGRAPH SO FAR AND THEN 209 FOR EVERY COMPLETE PARAGRAPH SO FAR. THIS GIVES THE POSITION IN THE STRINGS WHERE THE CHARACTERS HAVE TO BE POKED. NEXT PEEK INTO THE DISPLAY FILE AND POKE THE CONTENTS OF THE APPROPRIATE BYTE INTO THE ADDRESS CALCULATED EARLIER.

HERE IS THE CODE WHICH CHECKS TO SEE IF THE END OF THE PARAGRAPH HAS BEEN REACHED;

```
1300   FAST
1310   LET C = 1
1320   SCROLL
1330   FOR J = 1 TO 32
1340   POKE 16501 + J + L * 32 +
P * 209 , PEEK ( A - 33 + J )
1350   NEXT J
1360   LET L = L + 1
1370   IF L = 7 THEN GO SUB 930
1380   IF L = 7 THEN LET L = 1
1390   SLOW
1400   GO TO 1070
```

AND THATS ALL THERE IS TO STORING THE TEXT. THE REST OF THE PROGRAM IS CONCERNED WITH MAKING THE WRITING EASIER, MAKING EDITING POSSIBLE, ALLOWING THE TEXT TO BE READ THROUGH QUICKLY AND THEN PRINTED ON THE ZX PRINTER. IT IS USEFUL TO KNOW WHEN THE KEYS ARE CONTROLLING THE CURSOR AND WHEN THEY ARE ENTERING TEXT.

THE FIRST JOB IN THE NEXT SECTION IS TO PRINT A *CURSOR* MESSAGE WHENEVER THE EDIT MODE IS SELECTED. LINE 1500 ACHIEVES THIS AND LINE 1540 PRINTS EIGHT SPACES TO OBLITERATE THE SIGNAL ONCE PER CYCLE OF THE LOOP. DOING THIS MAKES THE CURSOR FLASH EVERY TIME A KEY IS PRESSED AND ALLOWS THE USER TO LEAVE THE *EDIT* LOOP WITHOUT LEAVING THE MESSAGE ON THE SCREEN.

```
1500   PRINT AT 20 , 16 ;
" CURSOR "
1510   IF INKEY$ <> " " THEN
GO TO 1510
1520   IF INKEY$ = " " THEN
GO TO 1520
1530   LET A$ = INKEY$
1540   PRINT AT 20 , 16 ;
"  eight spaces  "
1550   GO SUB 900
1560   POKE A + C , PEEK
( A + C ) - 128
```

LINES 1570 TO 1600 ADJUST THE POSITION OF THE CURSOR ALONG THE LINE. LINES 1610 TO 1670 MOVE THE CURSOR ONE PARAGRAPH BACK OR FORWARD OR MOVE IT DOWN A LINE. LINES 1680/90 CHECK FOR THE END OF A PARAGRAPH AND PRINT A NEW SET OF THREE IF NECESSARY. LINE 1700 REMOVES THE CURSOR FROM THE LAST POSITION WHEN IT IS NEEDED ELSEWHERE, LINE 1710 CHECKS TO SEE IF *WRITE* MODE HAS BEEN SELECTED AND, IF NOT, LINE 1720 SENDS THE MACHINE BACK FOR A NEW KEY STROKE.

```
1570   IF A$ = " 5 " THEN LET
C = C - 1
1580   IF A$ = " 8 " THEN LET
C = C + 1
1590   IF A$ = " 9 " THEN LET
C = C + 5
1600   IF C < 1 OR C > 32 THEN
LET C = 1
1610   IF A$ = " N " THEN LET
L = 1
1620   IF A$ = " N " THEN GO SUB
930
1630   IF A$ = " 7 " THEN LET
P = P - 2
1640   IF A$ = " 7 " THEN LET
L = 1
1650   IF A$ = " 7 " THEN GO SUB
930
1660   IF A$ = " 6 " THEN SCROLL
1670   IF A$ = " 6 " THEN LET
L = L + 1
1680   IF L = 7 THEN GO SUB 930
1690   IF L = 7 THEN LET L = 1
1700   POKE A + C , PEEK ( A +
C) + 128
1710   IF A$ = " > " THEN GO TO
1080
1720   GO TO 1500
```

NEXT IN THE LISTING IS THE INEVITABLE *MENU*. THE LINES NEED NO DOCUMENTATION.

```
2990   CLS
3000   PRINT TAB 7 ; '' WORD
JUGGLER ''
3010   PRINT
3020   PRINT '' KEY 1 TO WRITE
TEXT ''
3030   PRINT '' KEY 2 TO EDIT ''
3040   PRINT '' KEY 3 TO READ ''
3050   PRINT '' KEY 4 TO DELETE
A PARAGRAPH ''
3060   PRINT '' KEY 5 TO FILE
TEXT ''
3070   PRINT '' KEY 6 TO PRINT
TEXT ''
3100   INPUT A$
3110   IF A$ = '' 1 '' THEN GO TO
1000
3120   IF A$ = '' 2 '' THEN GO TO
3200
3130   IF A$ = '' 3 '' THEN GO TO
3500
3140   IF A$ = '' 4 '' THEN GO TO
4000
3150   IF A$ = '' 5 '' THEN GO TO
5000
3160   IF A$ = '' 6 '' THEN GO TO
3180   GO TO 2990
4500
```

WHEN *EDIT* IS SELECTED IT IS NECESSARY TO SELECT THE RIGHT PARAGRAPH.

```
3200   CLS
3210   PRINT TAB 10; " EDITING "
3220   PRINT AT 5 , 0 ; " KEY
PARAGRAPH NO "
3230   INPUT A
3240   LET P = A - 1
3250   LET A$ = " N "
3260   LET C = 1
3270   GO TO 1610
```

THE SIMPLEST WAY OF READING THE TEXT THROUGH IS TO PRINT THE FIRST THREE PARAGRAPHS, WAIT FOR A KEY STROKE AND THEN PRINT THE NEXT THREE. THIS IS THE METHOD USED BUT AN AUTOMATIC PRINTING ROUTINE MAY BE NEEDED. A FOR/ NEXT LOOP WHICH COUNTS UP TO 500 GIVES A SMOOTHER PAUSE THAN THE *PAUSE* STATEMENT. THE NUMBER TO BE COUNTED TO SHOULD BE FOUND BY EXPERIMENT. IF YOU WISH TO HAVE THIS FACILITY THE FOLLOWING LINES SHOULD REPLACE LINES 3520 TO 3540:

```
3520   FOR J = 1 TO 500
3530   NEXT J
3540   GO TO 3510
```

AND HERE IS THE STANDARD VERSION OF THE CODE:

```
3500   LET P = 2
3510   GO SUB 910
3520   IF INKEY$ = " " THEN GO
TO 3520
3530   LET P = P + 3
3540   GO TO 3510
```

DELETING A WHOLE PARAGRAPH AT A TIME MAY BE USEFUL. YOU MAY WISH TO CHANGE THE TEXT SO DRASTICALLY THAT DELETION WOULD BE THE EASIEST ACTION. THESE NEXT FEW LINES POKE ZERO INTO EACH BYTE IN THE STRINGS THAT THE SPECIFIED PARAGRAPH OCCUPIES. ONCE ONE HAS BEEN DELETED, THE OPTION IS GIVEN TO DELETE THE NEXT ONE AS WELL. TO SAFEGUARD AGAINST DELETING A PARAGRAPH BY ACCIDENT THE USER MUST ACTIVELY SIGNAL HIS AGREEMENT TO THE DELETION AND LINES 4050 AND 4070 SEE TO THIS.

```
4000   CLS
4010   PRINT TAB 10 ; "DELETING"
4020   PRINT
4030   PRINT " WHICH PARAGRAPH?"
4040   INPUT P
4050   PRINT " KEY D TO DELETE
PARAGRAPH * " ; P
4060   INPUT A$
4070   IF A$ <> " D " THEN GO TO
2990
4075   FAST
4080   FOR J = 1 TO 192
4090   POKE 16533 + J + P *
209 , 0
4100   NEXT J
4105   SLOW
4110   LET P = P + 1
4120   GO TO 4050
```

AND NOW, WHAT ALL THE CODE SO FAR HAS BEEN WORKING TOWARDS, PRINTING OUT THE TEXT THAT HAS BEEN ENTERED. TO AVOID PRINTING OUT BLANK PARAGRAPHS LINE 4510 ASKS FOR THE END OF THE PRINT RUN REQUIRED. LINE 4560 USES THE LOOP COUNTER TO CALCULATE THE LINE NUMBERS OF THE SUB-ROUTINES AND LINE 4570 USES THE PRINTER COMMAND *LPRINT* TO PRINT THE CONTENTS OF A$ ACCORDING TO THE SUB-ROUTINE SELECTED.

```
4500   CLS

4510   PRINT " KEY THE LAST

PARAGRAPH TO BE PRINTED "

4520   INPUT A

4530   CLS

4540   PRINT AT 10 , 10 ;

" PRINTING "

4550   FOR J = 1 TO A

4560   GO SUB J * 2 + 100

4570   LPRINT A$

4580   NEXT J

4600   PRINT AT 10 , 10 ;

" FINISHED "
4610   INPUT A$

4620   GO TO 2990
```

THE PROGRAM IS FINISHED WITH A SEGMENT WHICH SETS UP THE SAVE SEQUENCE AUTOMATICALLY AND SETS A$ TO THE NAME OF THE PROGRAM: MY OWN VERSION IS CALLED *WORD*. LINE 5040 ALLOWS THE COMPUTER TO START WORK ON THE PROGRAM AS SOON AS IT IS LOADED, YOU WILL NOT NEED TO USE *RUN* AND *NEW LINE*. THE FINAL REM STATEMENT

ACTS AS A LABEL SHOULD THE PROGRAM BE SENT INTO PROGRAM MODE BY A MISTAKEN USE OF THE BREAK KEY.

```
5000   CLS
TAPE "
5010   PRINT TAB 9 ; " START
TAPE " ; TAB 9 ; " KEY NEWLINE "
5020   INPUT A$
5030   CLS
5040   LET A$ = " WORD "
5050   SAVE A$
5060   GO TO 3000
6000   REM WORD JUGGLER
```

USING THE WORD JUGGLER

YOU WILL FIND TWO EXTRA PIECES OF HARDWARE VERY USEFUL; A PIECE OF BLACK TAPE TO SHOW WHERE THE END OF LINE 7 IS ON YOUR TV AND A PIECE OF PLASTICINE OR SIMILAR MATERIAL TO PUT ON THE BREAK KEY AS A REMINDER NOT TO USE IT TO WRITE A SPACE.

WHEN THE READABILITY CALCULATOR IS ADDED TO THE WORD JUGGLER, THE FULL STOP HAS A PARTICULAR SIGNIFICANCE. THE END OF A SENTENCE IS RECOGNISED BY THE ENTRY OF A STOP. THE USE OF A * . * IN ABBREVIATIONS AND NUMBERS WOULD CAUSE ERRORS IN THE ARITHMETIC SO SOME OTHER SYMBOL MUST BE USED. 1,01 IS USED IN EUROPE FOR 1.01 BUT ETC, LOOKS ODD AS A SUB STITUTE FOR ETC. SO AN ALTERNATIVE MUST BE FOUND. THE GRAPHIC CHARACTER OBTAINED BY KEYING (SHIFT 4) IS QUITE CLOSE TO A

STOP IN APPEARANCE, A BIT LARGE MAYBE BUT LESS CONFUSING THAN A COMMA. THE FOLLOWING LINE WILL SERVE A DOUBLE PURPOSE. IT WILL PROTECT YOU FROM THE DANGER OF USING INVERTED COMMAS BY MISTAKE AND GIVE YOU ACCESS TO THE ALTER NATIVE STOP:

```
1145 IF CODE A$=11 THEN LET
     A$=*(SHIFT 4)*
```

THIS SLOWS UP THE LOOP A LITTLE AND SO IT IS OFFERED AS AN OPT-IONAL EXTRA FOR INTERESTED READ-ERS. AND NOW THE MAIN OPTIONAL EXTRA, THE READABILITY CALCULA-TOR. THE FIRST SECTION FITS INTO THE ROUTINE WHICH COPIES THE COM PLETED LINES INTO THE STORAGE. THE CONTENTS OF THE STORES HOLD-ING THE LINE ARE STORED BY TURNS IN *R*. IF THE CHARACTER IS A LETTER OR A NUMBER THEN ONE IS ADDED TO *LT*. IF A STOP HAS BEEN ENTERED THEN ONE IS ADDED TO THE SENTENCES STORE, *ST*. SPACES ARE MORE DIFFICULT AS TWO OR MORE SPACES MIGHT BE LEFT AT THE END OF A LINE. A FLAG IS SET EACH TIME A SPACE APPEARS AND CANCELLED WHEN ANOTHER CHARACTER IS FOUND. IF THE FLAG IS ALREADY SET TO ONE WHEN A SPACE IS FOUND THEN THE NEW SPACE IS IGNORED. IF THE SPACE IS THE FIRST ONE IT SIGNIFIES THE END OF A WORD SO ONE IS ADDED TO *WD*. HERE ARE THE LINES TO BE ADDED:

```
1325  LET S=0
1331  LET R=PEEK (A-33+J)
1332   IF R>=28 AND R<=63
      THEN LET LT=LT+1
```

```
1333  IF R=27 THEN LET
      ST=ST+1
1334  IF R=0 AND S=0
      THEN LET WD=WD+1
1335  IF R=0 THEN LET
      S=1
1336  IF R<>0 THEN LET
      S=0
1340   POKE 16501+J+L*32
      +P* 209, R
```

THE FINAL LINE IS AN EDITED VERSION OF THE ORIGINAL WHICH SAVES A FEW BYTES.

HAVING ESTABLISHED HOW MANY SENTENCES, WORDS AND LETTERS HAVE BEEN WRITTEN, THE NEXT JOB IS TO USE THIS INFORMATION TO CALCULATE THE READING DIFFICULTY. THE INFORMATION GIVEN IS THE NUMBER OF WORDS PER SENTENCE AND THE NUMBER OF LETTERS PER WORD. THE DATA IS DISPLAYED ON LINES 21 AND 22. THIS LINE GETS THE DATA INTO PLACE:

```
920  PRINT AT 20,0;"WDS/
     SEN"; INT (10*WD/ST)
     /10,,"LET/WD"; INT
     (10*LT/WD)/10
```

THIS WILL PRINT THE INFORMATION TO ONE DECIMAL PLACE AND WHEN THE SENTENCES OR WORDS GET TOO LONG IT IS TIME TO SIMPLIFY THE TEXT. IN ORDER TO SEE HOW WELL THE ATTEMPT IS SUCCEEDING IT IS NECESSARY TO RE-SET THE READABILITY CALCULATOR FROM TIME TO TIME. BEFORE GIVING THE CODE TO DO THIS JOB SOME SPACE WILL HAVE TO BE MADE FOR THE EXTRA LINES. THREE OF THE STORAGE PARAGRAPHS WILL HAVE TO GO TO MAKE ROOM.

AFTER DELETING THESE, LINE 911 WILL HAVE TO BE CHANGED SO THAT THE PROGRAM STOPS IN THE RIGHT PLACE.

```
911  IF P=55 THEN GO TO 2990
```

AND NOW THE CODE WHICH RE-SETS THE READABILITY:

```
3080  PRINT "KEY 7 TO RE-SET
      READABILITY"
3170  IF A$="7" THEN GO TO
      4700
3180  GO TO 2990
4610  PRINT " KEY NEWLINE "
4615  INPUT A$
4620  GO TO 2990
4700  LET WD=1
4710  LET ST=WD
4720  LET LT=WD
4730  CLS
4740  PRINT "READABILITY
      RE-SET"
4750  PRINT "KEY NEWLINE"
4760  INPUT A$
4770  GO TO 2990
```

A FLOW CHART OF THE READABILITY CALCULATOR IS GIVEN AT THE END OF THE CHAPTER.

A LITTLE PRACTICE WILL SOON GET YOU USED TO THE WORD JUGGLER SO LOAD IT INTO THE MACHINE AND START WRITING WHILE BEARING THE FOLLOWING TIPS IN MIND. FIRST OF ALL, DEVELOP A RHYTHMIC STYLE OF TYPING AND KEY IN DOUBLE LETTERS AT THE SAME RATE THAT YOU KEY IN THE OTHERS. THE STRIP OF BLACK TAPE ON THE SCREEN SAVES A LOT OF CODE AND GIVES YOU A FULL 32 CHARACTERS TO THE LINE. TO PRINT

AN END OF LINE WARNING SEEMED NOT TO BE WORTH THE TROUBLE. IT IS SURPRISING HOW EFFECTIVE THE TAPE IS AND HOW THE LUMP OF PLA-STICINE STOPS YOU USING *BREAK* FOR A SPACE. THE END OF A LINE IS THE MOST AWKWARD PART OF THE WHOLE PACKAGE BECAUSE A MISTAKE THERE IS MORE DIFFICULT TO CORR-ECT. THE PROCEDURE IS:

1) GO INTO EDIT MODE.
2) KEY 7 FOR THE LAST PARAGRAPH.
3) KEY 6 UNTIL THE LINE WITH THE MISTAKE IS REACHED.
4) KEY 8 OR 9 UNTIL THE MISTAKE IS COVERED BY THE CURSOR.
5) GO BACK TO WRITE MODE AND CORRECT THE MISTAKE.

ALL OF WHICH IS NOT AS BAD AS IT SOUNDS BUT ANNOYING. MAKE YOUR MISTAKES IN THE MIDDLE OF THE LINE, THEY ARE EASIER. MISTAKES ARE BOUND TO HAPPEN AND THE CORR ECTION ROUTINE IS; GO BACK INTO EDIT MODE, MOVE THE CURSOR TO THE MISTAKE, GO BACK TO WRITE MODE AND CARRY ON TYPING AS IF NOTHING HAD HAPPENED.

HITTING THE BREAK KEY BY MISTAKE WILL SOON BECOME A RARE EVENT BUT FOR THE MOMENT, HERE IS WHAT TO DO. THE SIGNAL IS THE REPORT CODE * D * BUT, BEING ENGROSSED IN YOUR WORK YOU WILL NOT NOTICE UNTIL THE PROGRAM REPLACES YOUR TEXT ON THE SCREEN. EITHER KEY GOTO 3000 OR KEY CONTINUE. GO TO 3000 WILL REQUIRE THAT YOU KNOW THE PARAGRAPH NUMBER. USING CONTINUE WILL MEAN HAVING TO GO INTO EDIT MODE BEFORE MOVING TO THE NEXT PARAGRAPH TO PRINT

TEXT ON THE SCREEN. ONCE TEXT IS REPRINTED THE CURSOR CONTROL KEYS SOON MOVE YOU BACK TO THE PRINT POSITION. AGAIN, THIS SOUNDS MUCH MORE INVOLVED THAN IT IS IN PRACTICE.

THE LAST POINT THAT NEEDS MAKING IS THAT EDITING IS ONLY PERMANENT IF THE LINE BEING EDITED IS COPIED INTO THE STORAGE STRINGS. CORRECTING THE MISTAKE AND THEN GOING INTO EDIT MODE AGAIN TO MOVE ON TO THE NEXT CORRECTION ONLY ALTERS THE TEXT ON THE SCREEN. AFTER MAKING A CORRECTION, USE THE CURSOR KEYS IN EDIT MODE TO MOVE TO THE END OF THE LINE OR, IF IT IS MORE CONVENIENT, TYPE OVER THE CHARACTERS AGAIN. WHEN AT THE END OF THE LINE, MAKE SURE YOU ARE IN WRITE MODE AND THEN TYPE THE LAST SPACE OR CHARACTER AND WAIT THE SECOND NEEDED TO COPY THE LINE. THE CORRECTION WILL NOW BE PERMANENT, AT LEAST UNTIL YOU EDIT THE LINE AGAIN.

IF YOUR WORK NEEDS THE ATTENTION OF THE READABILITY CALCULATOR BE PREPARED TO WAIT A LITTLE LONGER FOR THE COMPLETED LINES TO BE COPIED INTO THE STORAGE STRINGS. THE COUNTING IS DONE IN THE *COPY* LOOP AND TAKES A LITTLE TIME. DONT FORGET TO RESET THE CALCULATOR BEFORE USING THE PROGRAM. THE VARIABLES WILL NOT BE SET UP UNLESS THIS IS DONE. JUST REMEMBER TO KEY 7 AT THE MENU THE FIRST TIME.

FLOW CHART FOR READING AGE CALCULATOR

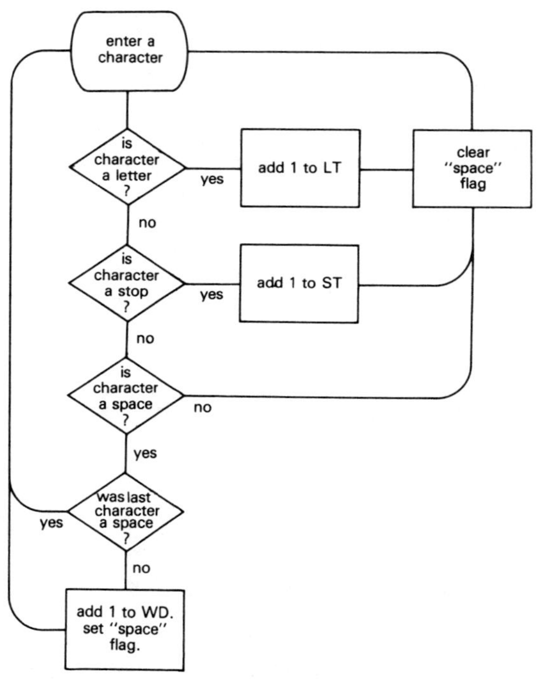

Figure 4.1 Flow chart for reading age calculator

FLOW CHART FOR WORD JUGGLER

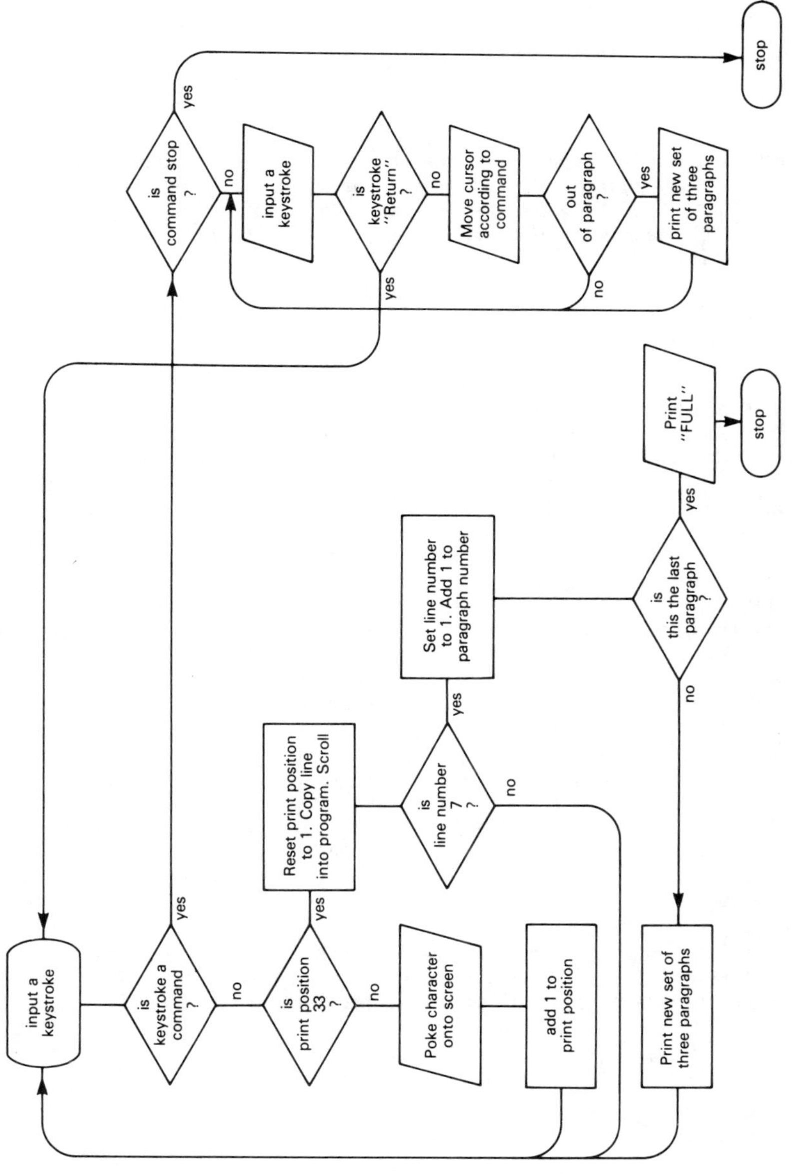

Figure 4.2 Flow chart for word juggler

5 *Money*

NOTE *In this chapter and elsewhere in the book, readers in the USA, Australia, and other countries will have to substitute "$" for "£" where money is dealt with. Otherwise the program will not, of course, require changes for any decimal currencies.*

Dealing with money matters in a reasonably efficient way means performing some very simple chores regularly. These chores include storing many pieces of paper and then remembering where they were put, remembering when payments fall due and how much must be paid, recording each movement of cash into and out of the accounts and adding up all the figures. These all sound so simple, but there can be few of us who have carried out these tasks faultlessly for any length of time. Many of these jobs can be computerised. This in itself will not work miracles but a lot of time and frustration may be saved as a result. Arithmetic is likely to be more reliable and there should no longer be occasions when a standing order is forgotten. This should avoid those wild, unjustified spending sprees which are so often followed by a letter from the bank manager.

These tasks and problems will be familiar to the organisers of household accounts but the same ones crop up in business as well. As the problems are similar wherever money has to be organised, it would be useful to write a standard system to allow the computer to do all the tasks in a standard way. The same system can then be used in each program which has to deal with money. It is a simple matter to load the system into the ZX81 before starting to write the main program. The cash handling system which follows consists of a series of subroutines which can be called as necessary by the main part of the program. The subroutines do the following jobs:

a) load an amount of cash into the machine;

b) add cash to or subtract it from a balance held in the computer,

c) print a balance and draw attention to an overdrawn account,

d) load a date into the machine and

e) check all information as it is keyed in and give an opportunity to correct any typing mistakes.

Once confidence in the system develops, the programmer can forget about the financial detail and concentrate on the main job that the program has to do.

Programs which rely heavily on subroutines to do the donkey work can suffer from screen overflow if the text that builds up on the screen is not cleared regularly. All the routines in this system clear the screen automatically and the only one which leaves anything on the screen at all is the routine which prints a balance. This feature should avoid the "screen full" messages and improve the presentation of programs using the system. Figure 5.1 shows how the main program calls the routines and how some of the routines call others.

SUBROUTINE A, LOADING AN AMOUNT INTO THE MACHINE

The cash handling system has to be by-passed until it is called and so the first line is:

```
1       GO TO 200
```

The system only occupies lines 10 to 75 but the programs into which the system is to be built will probably have subroutines of their own and so space has to be left for these. Don't worry if the line numbers do not work through quite regularly. All the lines are there, the gaps are left to accommodate lines which are present in the software which accompanies this work. A cash handling system for the ZX80 is available on tape and this has to be much more involved to get the earlier machine to deal with money as smoothly as the ZX81 and so more lines are needed. If the cash handling system is to be at all standard then all variations of it should have the same addresses for the GO SUB calls.

```
10      PRINT " KEY THE AMOUNT " ; TAB 20 ; " EG.£ 49.04 "
11      INPUT AJ
12      CLS
13      PRINT " £ " ; AJ
14      GO SUB 70     (a routine to check the typing)
15      IF A$ <> " C " THEN GO TO 10 (C means the typing
                                        is OK)
16      RETURN
```

The 49.04 in line 10 can be printed in inverse video to highlight the style of presentation which the ZX81 will find acceptable. The need for the leading zero in four pence has to be emphasised. The variable " AJ " is used for the AdJusting amount, leaving " A " free for use in the main program. The next routine in the ZX81 version of the system starts at line thirty.

```
30      LET AJ = AJ * -1
35      LET BL = BL + AJ
36      RETURN
```

To add an amount to the balance use the command GO SUB 35. To subtract some cash from the balance use GO SUB 30 which multiplies the amount by minus one before adding it. The routine which prints out the balance after the adjustments starts at line forty-five.

```
45      IF BL < 0 THEN PRINT " OVERDRAWN BY * " ;
46      PRINT " £ " ; INT ( BL * 100 + .5 ) / 100 ;
47      IF BL >= 0 THEN PRINT " * IN CREDIT "
48      PRINT
49      RETURN
```

You will remember that " * " means a space but there is much more than this that needs explanation in this section. The message that indicates the credit or overdraft status of the account is printed in different orders to emphasise an overdraft as required in item " c " in the specification for the system. And now, the difficult bit. If a program using the system calculates interest then it is likely that the balance will hold values rather like: 103.0488394 which would be very messy if it were printed on the screen. For most purposes, values printed to the nearest penny are needed. Lets follow through line 46 and see what happens to this value along the way.

a) PRINT " £ " ; INT (BL * 100 + .5) / 100

b) PRINT " £ " ; INT (10304.88394 + . 5) / 100

c) PRINT " £ " ; INT (10305.38394) / 100

d) PRINT " £ " ; 10305 / 100

e) £103.05

which is the value held in BL, printed to the nearest penny. The next section starts at line sixty, deals with dates and is much simpler.

```
60      PRINT " KEY THE DATE, DAY NO. FIRST "
61      INPUT D1
62      PRINT " NEXT THE MONTH NO. "
63      INPUT D2
64      PRINT " THE LAST 2 DIGITS OF THE YEAR? "
65      INPUT D3
66      PRINT D1 ; " / " ; D2 ; " / " ; D3
67      GO SUB 70            (checks for typing errors)
68      IF AS <> " C " THEN GO TO 60      (C means OK)
69      RETURN
```

And now the routine called by the others in the system as well as the main program, the typing mistake routine.

```
70      PRINT
71      PRINT " KEY C IF THIS IS OK , OTHERWISE NEWLINE "
72      INPUT A$
73      CLS
74      RETURN
```

The CLS at line 73 does a lot of work keeping the display tidy. Because this routine is called by others before they return control to the main program, there is no need for CLS commands in the other routines. Line 71 is the first one which asks the ZX81 to print a line which contains more than thirty-two characters and, as written here, would be very untidy as the line would end half way through a word. Throughout the rest of the book, I could put in the spaces necessary to keep the display neat but this would make the listings difficult to read and, anyway, there is a better way to do the job. As you key in characters to make up a long print line, notice where the first quotes character comes on the line. Each line of screen print will end under this character. If you are half way through a word go back to the beginning of the word and put in a space or two to move the start of the word to the start of the next line. Remember that the cursor occupies a space and has to be allowed for and also that it is cheaper to start another PRINT line if you put in more than five spaces.

To print out that sentence which contains all the letters of the alphabet and not split a word, follow the following procedure. As with so many of these, it is very much more simple to do at the machine than it is to understand when read straight from the page.

```
10 PRINT "THE QUICK RED FOX JUMP
ED OVER THE LAZY BROWN DOG"
```

prints as:

```
THE QUICK RED FOX JUMPED OVER TH
E LAZY BROWN DOG
```

Whereas:

```
10 PRINT "THE QUICK RED FOX JUMPED
ED OVER **THE LAZY BROWN DOG"
```

with its extra space and the " T "s in the two " THE "s directly above one another prints as:

```
THE QUICK RED FOX JUMPED OVER
THE LAZY BROWN DOG
```

If you practice this simple technique a few times and bear it in mind when working with long print lines all the screen presentation should be of professional rather than amateur quality.

The cash handling system will form the basis of the next two programs. You can save it onto tape and then load it in when you are ready to start work on one of the listings.

CASH HANDLING SYSTEM, VARIABLES USED

AJ	Adjusting amount of cash
A$	General signal
BL	Balance
D1	Day number
D2	Month number
D3	Year number

CASH HANDLING SYSTEM LAYOUT

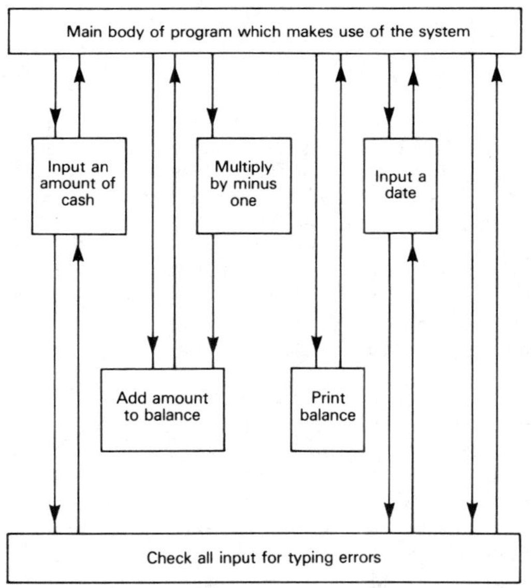

Figure 5.1 Cash handling system layout

6 *Personal Finances*

This program, which will run all your household accounts, will save you time but this is not the most important benefit which the package offers. Since it was pressed into service in our home, the family finances have not been at the mercy of my far from perfect memory. I no longer have to remember if I have deducted last month's standing orders or if I have already added this month's salary to the balance. These jobs are done automatically as they fall due. I don't have to remember where the old documents are, I just have to remember where the tape is. The arithmetic is better too.

It is all very well, writing a program to keep tabs on your accounts, but it is not very helpful to produce something which costs more time and effort to run than it saves. It might be nice to store the detail of every movement of cash into and out of the account but this would cost a lot of memory. Memory cost means an increase in the LOAD and SAVE time and it is pointless using a program which takes six minutes to load and another six to save, all to save five minutes on a calculator. The following list of jobs can be coded into a program which will take only ninety seconds to load.

JOBS TO BE AUTOMATED

1) Filing details of regular payments and the dates they fall due.
2) Remembering which cheque has to be deducted next.
3) Remembering which is the next paying-in slip to be added.
4) Deciding when salary cheques must be added and standing orders deducted.

5) Allowing for the possibility of special payments into and out of the account.

6) Making provision for changes in the standing orders.

There were few problems when these jobs were coded into BASIC. The most difficult task was getting the ZX81 to decide when to add in the salary and deduct the standing orders. To make the job as simple as possible, it was decided that the orders were to be deducted on the same day of the month as the salary was credited. I have used the 25th of the month as payday. The machine decides when to ask the amount of the pay cheque on the basis of two dates held in the memory. The date of the previous run is remembered and the new date is requested soon after the program is loaded. The problem is a complex one to solve but even more difficult to describe succinctly. The flow chart which helped sort out the problem will be given later, next to the section of code which it covers.

The first part of the program is the cash handling system which can be loaded into the ZX81 from the cassette and used as a basis for this program. The next section after the cash handling system is the main menu which will appear on the screen as soon as the program is loaded:

```
200    CLS
210    PRINT " PERSONAL FINANCES "
220    PRINT " ________ "  (underlining of your choice)
230    PRINT " TO UPDATE THE BALANCE        KEY U "
240    PRINT " TO SET UP THE SYSTEM         KEY S "
250    PRINT " TO CHANGE STANDING ORDERS    KEY C "
260    PRINT " TO FILE                      KEY F "
270    INPUT A$
280    IF A$ = " U " THEN GO TO 2000
282    IF A$ = " S " THEN GO TO 300
284    IF A$ = " C " THEN GO TO 1200
286    IF A$ = " F " THEN GO TO 3000
290    GO TO 200
```

Line 290 sends the machine back to set up the menu again if the keystroke made by the user does not correspond to any of the choices on offer.

The next section of code is optional and it is a very large section. It enables the computer to set itself up during the first run but is never used again and takes up a lot of space. An alternative and much simpler method of setting the system up is given after the listing but this demands the use of direct commands and inexperienced users may feel unable to cope with this. If you are writing for inexperienced friends or fellow club members who only feel comfortable, interacting with the ZX81, while it is running normally and speaking English, then key in these lines. The next section for those who feel able to cope with giving the ZX81 direct commands starts at line 1200, but all users will need the subroutines which start at line 80 and part of these are listed in the setting up section on page 79.

If you decide not to include the setting up section you may well find the rest of the listing clearer if you have read "setting up" through. A lot of detail on the data storage and retrieval is included in the text and an understanding of this will be useful for material in later chapters. The explanation on page 78 is particularly important.

SETTING UP THE SYSTEM

```
300    CLS
310    LET BL = 0    (all variables must be set up and
                      this is as good a way as any)
330    LET D$ = " MONTH DUE "
340    PRINT " ARE YOU IN CREDIT OR OVERDRAWN AT THE BANK ?
C / O "
350    INPUT B$
360    GO SUB 10
370    IF B$ = " O " THEN GO SUB 30
380    IF B$ = " C " THEN GO SUB 35
390    IF B$ <> " C " AND B$ <> " O " THEN GO TO 300
```

The program is written to allow up to ten standing orders to be paid monthly, ten to be paid quarterly and ten annual ones. The details are to be stored in arrays and so these have to be dimensioned.

```
400    DIM Q(10)
410    DIM N(10)
420    DIM M(10)
```

And now to fill these up. Two loops will be used, one under the control of counter " K " which will decide which of the arrays is to be filled and the other controlled by " J " which identifies the element to be filled next. The working of the section is outlined in the diagram.

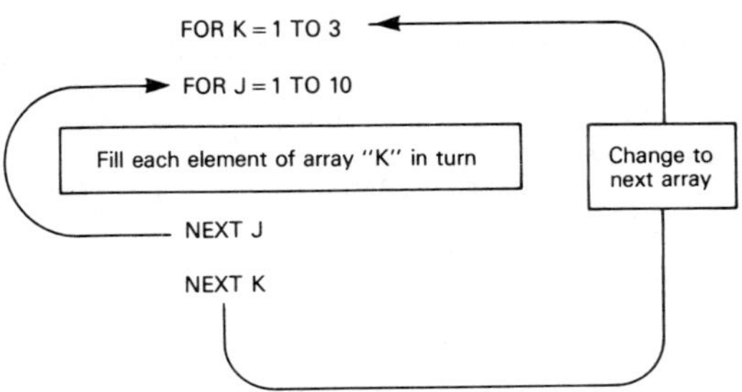

And here are the lines of BASIC that do the work:

```
430    FOR K = 1 TO 3
440    FOR J = 1 TO 10
450    IF K = 1 THEN PRINT " MONTHLY " ;
460    IF K = 2 THEN PRINT " QUARTERLY " ;
470    IF K = 3 THEN PRINT " ANNUAL " ;
480    PRINT " * STANDING ORDER NO. * " ; J
490    GO SUB 10   (calls for an amount of cash)
500    IF AJ = 0 THEN NEXT K
```

This section prints a series of requests. The ZX81 asks the amount of each of the standing orders in turn. If the user responds with zero then the machine knows that all the standing orders due monthly have been entered and so goes on to the quarterly ones. If ten quarterly orders are keyed in the computer will move automatically on to the annual orders after the tenth. The ZX81 uses the value held in " K " to decide what to do with the figures being fed in.

```
510    IF K = 2 THEN GO TO 590 (which looks after the
                                quarterlies)
520    IF K = 3 THEN GO TO 690 (which sorts out the annual
                                orders)
530    IF K = 4 THEN GO TO 800 (which prints a table of the
                                orders)
```

```
540     LET M(J) = AJ  (this happens when K equals one)
570     NEXT J
580     NEXT K
```

If K doesn't equal two or three or even four then it must be set to one so the payment amount is fed into array (M), element (J). The array holds the information on the monthly orders.

```
590     PRINT D$           (prints " month due ")
620     INPUT A
630     PRINT TAB 8 ; " MONTH * " ; A
640     GO SUB 70          (typing mistake?)
650     IF A$ <> " C " THEN GO TO 590
```

Having checked the typing at 70 and decided to accept or reject the figure, the next job is to store the amount of this quarterly payment and the month during which it must be paid. Both pieces of information are stored in the same variable using a technique which will be used more and more later in the book. This technique is introduced here in a small way so that you will already be familiar with it when it is pushed to its limit in the chapter on "Bulk Storage". It is safe to assume that very few readers will have regular payments in excess of £999.99 and so if the amount of the standing order is divided by 1000 then the result will be less than one. If your quarterly rates bill is £100 then the array element that stores it will hold 0.1. If the bill was £103.75 then the value stored would be 0.10375. All the information is there but it is there in miniature. If the month number of the next payment date is added to the element then, for a December bill the value held will be 12.10375. To find the month just take the integer value. To find the amount is a little more involved but here goes:

1) take the integer value and multiply by 100000, call this A
2) multiply the value in the element by 100000 and call this B
3) subtract A from B and divide by 100

And here goes again, in figures this time:

1) 12 * 100000 = 1200 000	A = 1 200 000
2) 12.10375 * 100000 = 1210 375	B = 1 210 375
3) A - B = 10375	10375 / 100 = 103.75

This seems a little cumbersome here but it will save a lot of space and there is a very neat method of extracting the information later, but this little taste will do for now.

```
660     LET Q(J) = AJ / 1000 + A
670     NEXT J
680     NEXT K
```

will not seem quite so strange after the explanation. The technique saves quite a lot of space. If the month and the amount of the payment were to be stored in separate variables then at least 100 extra bytes would be needed for the storage. A similar segment of program follows. This feeds values into the array (N) which holds the annual standing orders.

```
690     PRINT D$                        (prints " month due? ")
710     INPUT A
730     LET N(J) = AJ / 1000 + A
740     NEXT J
750     NEXT K
```

At the end of the loop, controlled by " K ", the counter will be set to 4 and so the loop will not cycle again. The computer recognises this as a signal at line 530 and so goes off to line 800 where there is a routine which displays the state of the standing orders.

```
800     CLS
810     GO SUB 80                       (prints out the orders)
820     GO SUB 70                       (typing errors?)
830     IF A$ <> " C " THEN GO TO 400
840     CLS
```

Going to 400 at line 830 has the effect of re-DIMensioning the arrays and this automatically clears any arrays with the same variable name.

Having mentioned the routine at line 80, now is the time to give the listing:

```
80      PRINT " STANDING ORDERS "
81      LET Z = 100000   (this saves typing later on)
```

```
82      PRINT " NO. " ; TAB 4 ; " £ MONTH " ; TAB 13 ;
" £ QUARTER " ; TAB 24 ; " £ ANNUAL "
83      FOR J = 1 TO 10
84      PRINT J ; TAB 4 ; M(J) ; TAB 13 ; ( INT ( Q(J) * Z +
.5 ) - INT Q(J) * Z ) / 100 ; TAB 20 ; INT Q(J) ; TAB 24 ;
( INT ( N(J) * Z + .5 ) - INT N(J) * Z ) / 100 ; TAB 30 ;
INT N(J)
85      NEXT J
86      RETURN
```

Line 84 is very complex but it would be even worse if it were not for line 81 which avoids lots of " 100000s ". The explanation of the storage and retrieval method which was given earlier will help with the understanding of this line.

Line 900 starts a segment which sets up another three variables to hold another date. This is the date which will be remembered from one run to the next and which will help decide which payments are due since the program was used last.

```
900     GO SUB 60          (reads in a date from the keyboard)
910     LET D4 = D1
920     LET D5 = D2        (to copy the date into the
                            other variables)
930     LET D6 = D3
940     CLS
```

After which is a straightforward part of the program which loads in the details of the current cheque book and paying-in book:

```
1000    CLS
1010    PRINT " KEY THE NUMBER OF YOUR CHEQUE BOOK "
1020    INPUT C
1030    PRINT C
1040    PRINT " NOW THE NEXT CHEQUE NO. "
1050    INPUT C1
1060    PRINT C1
1070    PRINT " NEXT THE LAST CHEQUE NO. IN THE BOOK "
1080    INPUT C2
1090    PRINT C2
```

```
1100    PRINT " AND THE NEXT PAYING-IN SLIP NO. "
1110    INPUT C3            (slip no.)
1120    PRINT C3
1130    GO SUB 70           (typing errors?)
1140    IF A$ <> " C " THEN GO TO 1000
1150    GO TO 200
```

This is the end of the setting up routine and, once used it can be deleted.

At the outset it was mentioned that the standing orders could not remain fixed at the same level for ever and so a routine which allows amendments must be written. The lines, starting at 1200, make use of the subroutine at line 80 to print out the S.O. chart for updating.

```
1200    CLS
1210    PRINT " REVISING"        (to get the headings right)
1220    GO SUB 80                (print out the S.O. chart)
1230    PRINT
1240    PRINT " WHICH S.O.? "
1250    INPUT J
1260    PRINT J
1270    PRINT " MONTH (1) QUARTER ( 2) OR YEAR (3) ? "
1280    INPUT A
1290    CLS
1300    PRINT " GIVE REVISED FIGURE "
1310    GO SUB 10                (input an amount of cash)
```

The ZX81 now has all the information it needs to select the correct array element and load the data in. The next two lines select the appropriate loading routine:

```
1320    IF A = 2 THEN GO TO 1380
1330    IF A = 3 THEN GO TO 1430
```

If " A " is anything else it must be 1 for a monthly standing order and so the next line deals with this case.

```
1340    LET M(J) = AJ
1350    GO TO 200                      (back to the menu)
1380    PRINT D$                       (month due?)
1390    INPUT A
1400    LET Q(J) = AJ / 1000 + A       (both data into the same
                                        element)
1410    GO TO 200
1430    PRINT D$
1440    INPUT A
1450    LET N(J) = AJ / 1000 + A
1460    GO TO 200                      (back to the menu)
```

Now, down to regular business:

```
2000    CLS
2010    PRINT " TRANSACTIONS SINCE * " ; D4 ; " / " ; D5 ;
" / " ; D6
2020    PRINT
2030    GO SUB 60
2040    IF ( D3 - D6 ) * 365 + ( D2 - D5 ) * 30 + D1 - D4
< 0 THEN GO TO 2030
```

This last line prevents journeys backwards in time. All sorts of difficulties would arise if this were possible. Salaries would be paid once and counted in twice. If interest were to be calculated then the new date would never be reached by the loop which adds in the interest so the machine would cycle endlessly. The line calculates the number of days that have past and refuses to go on if the result is negative.

The next section was a little more difficult to write and the flow chart which was used is shown in Figure 6.2. Read the next section of BASIC and the flow chart together.

```
2050    PRINT D1 ; " / " ; D2 ; " / " ; D3
2060    IF D5 = D2 and D6 = D3 THEN GO TO 2180
2070    IF D4 < 25 THEN GO SUB 2130
2080    LET D4 = 1
2090    LET D5 = D5 + 1
2100    IF D5 > 12 THEN LET D6 = D6 + 1
```

```
2110    IF D5 > 12 THEN LET D5 = D5 - 12
2120    GO TO 2060              (left hand loop on flow chart)
2130    PRINT " KEY SALARY FOR MONTH * " ; D5 ; " / " ; D6
2140    GO SUB 10               (calls for an amount of cash)
2150    GO SUB 35               (adds it to the balance)
```

Having decided which month's salary to load in, the ZX81 goes on to decide which standing orders are due. We are in the middle of a short subroutine which starts at line 2130. This routine calls three others, one of which has not yet been listed. The routine at line 90 is the one which decides about the standing orders. The listing of this routine follows on directly from the end of this present section.

```
2160    GO SUB 90
2170    RETURN
2180    IF D4 > 24 OR D1 < 25 THEN GO TO 2200  (next section)
2190    GO SUB 2130                            (calls for salary)

90      FOR J = 1 TO 10
91      LET AJ = M(J)
92      GO SUB 30               (deducts all the monthly orders)
93      NEXT J
95      FOR J = 1 TO 10
96      GO TO 120                              (payment due yet?)
97      LET AJ = ( Q(J) - INT Q(J)) * 1000 (loads amount due)
98      GO SUB 30                              (deducts from bal.)
99      NEXT J
100     FOR J = 1 TO 10
101     IF INT N(J) <> D5 THEN GO TO 104   (payment due?)
102     LET AJ = ( N(J) - INT N(J)) * 1000 (loads amount due)
103     GO SUB 30                              (deducts from bal.)
104     NEXT J
105     RETURN
```

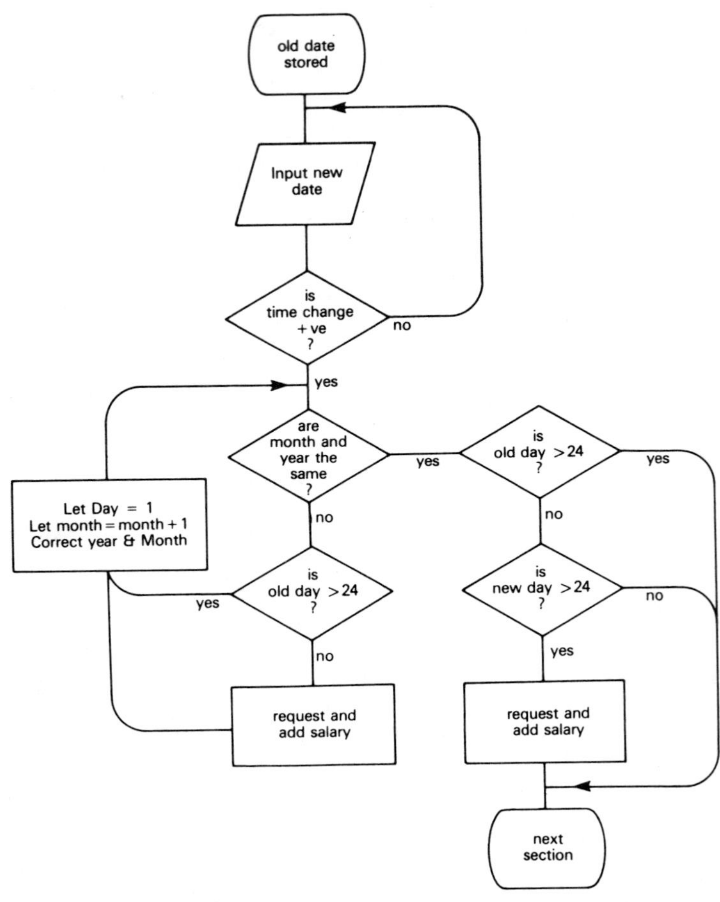

Figure 6.2 To add or not to add this month's salary

You may remember that only one of the months on which quarterly standing orders have to be paid was fed into the array. The section of program at line 120 uses this one month number to check that one of the other three months hasn't come up. If the present month number, held in the machine, is one of the four on which the payment must be made then the computer is sent to line 97 and deducts the payment from the balance. On any other month this section is by-passed and control is sent to line 99. The annual payments are easier. They have to be paid only when " INT N(J) " equals the present month number.

```
120    LET A = INT Q(J)
130    IF D5 = A OR D5 = A + 3 OR D5 = A + 6 OR D5 = A + 9
OR D5 = A - 3 OR D5 = A - 6 OR D5 = A - 9 THEN GO TO 97
140    LET A = 0              (just to keep the variables tidy)
150    GO TO 99
```

The rest of the listing is simplicity itself after that lot. First, all the cheques that have been written since the last time the balance was calculated have to be deducted. If a value of zero is entered then the ZX81 asks if the cheque is a cancelled one. If the answer is " NO " then it takes the input as a signal that the last cheque has been dealt with and goes on to ask about paying-in slips.

```
2200   CLS
2210   GO SUB 45            (to print the balance in the a/c)
2220   PRINT " CHEQUE BOOK NO. * " ; C
2230   PRINT " KEY THE VALUE OF CHEQUE NO. * " ; C1
2240   GO SUB 10            (to ask how much)
2250   GO SUB 30            (to deduct this much from the bal.)
2260   IF AJ = 0 THEN GO TO 2450   (cancelled cheque check)
2270   IF C1 = C2 THEN PRINT " IF YOU HAVE DETAILS OF BOOK "
2280   IF C1 = C2 THEN PRINT C + 1; " * THEN KEY D ,
OTHERWISE KEY NEWLINE "
2290   IF C1 = C2 THEN INPUT A$
2300   IF C1 = C2 AND A$ = " D " THEN GO TO 2340
2310   IF C1 = C2 THEN GO TO 2475
```

All of which needs a word or two of explanation. If C1 equals C2 then the next cheque is the last in the book. If the next book has arrived from the bank then the details can be fed in after keying

" D ". If, on the other hand, the bank are late in sending your new book, you cannot have written any of the cheques in it so the present run can continue. C1 is left unchanged so that the request for new book details will be printed during the next run.

```
2320   LET C1 = C1 + 1          (next cheque)
2330   GO TO 2200               (round again)
2340   LET C = C + 1            (next book)
2350   CLS
2360   PRINT " KEY THE FIRST CHEQUE NO. IN BOOK * " ; C
2370   INPUT C1
2380   PRINT C1
2390   PRINT " NOW THE LAST "
2400   INPUT C2
2410   PRINT C2
2420   GO SUB 70                   (typing mistakes?)
2430   IF A$ <> " C " THEN GO TO 2350
2440   GO TO 2200  (asks amount of first cheque in new book)
```

Next comes the " cancelled cheque " routine:

```
2450   PRINT " IF THAT WAS A CANCELLED CHEQUE KEY C
OTHERWISE KEY NEWLINE "
2460   INPUT A$
2470   IF A$ = " C " THEN LET C1 = C1 + 1
2475   CLS
2480   IF A$ = " C " THEN GO TO 2200  (amount of next cheque)
```

Now that all the possibilities are covered we can go on to ask about all the paying-in slips that have been written. The balance is written at this stage so the first line is:

```
2490   GO SUB 45                        (prints balance)
2500   PRINT " PAYMENTS INTO ACCOUNT "
2510   PRINT
2520   PRINT " KEY VALUE OF PAYING-IN SLIP NO. * " ; C3
2530   GO SUB 10                        (load amount)
2540   IF AJ = 0 THEN GO TO 2600  (same escape signal)
```

```
2550   GO SUB 35                         (adds this time)
2560   LET C3 = C3 + 1
2570   GO TO 2500                        (round again)
```

And on to the special payments into or out of the account which are not made via the cheque or paying-in book:

```
2600   CLS
2610   GO SUB 45                         (prints balance)
2620   PRINT " ANY SPECIAL PAYOUTS? Y/N "
2630   INPUT A$
2640   IF A$ <> " Y " THEN GO TO 2690
2650   GO SUB 10                         (load amount)
2660   GO SUB 30                         (deduct it)
2670   GO TO 2600                        (any more?)
2690   CLS
2700   PRINT " ANY SPECIAL DEPOSITS? Y/N "
2710   INPUT A$
2720   IF A$ <> " Y " THEN GO TO 200          (the main menu)
2730   GO SUB 10                              (load amount)
2740   GO SUB 35                              (add it)
2750   GO TO 2690                             (any more?)
```

Finally, the auto start routine after the final balance has been printed:

```
3000   CLS
3010   PRINT TAB 8 ; " FINAL BALANCE "
3020   PRINT
3030   GO SUB 45                              (prints balance)
3040   PRINT AT 10 , 10 ; " START TAPE "
3045   PRINT TAB 10 ; " KEY NEWLINE "
3050   INPUT A$
3060   LET D4 = D1  }
3070   LET D5 = D2  }  (sets the date of the "last run" for
                   }   next time)
3080   LET D6 = D3  }
```

```
3090   CLS
3100   SAVE "CASH"
3110   GO TO 200
```

As listed, the program will get off to a flying start the very first time it is loaded into the ZX81. If, however, you have omitted the setting up routine there is another job to be done before the program will run without crashing.

SETTING UP PROCEDURE

First of all, delete lines 240 and 282 from the menu section and then key in these commands without line numbers. The ZX81 will execute these right away and the information will be remembered from one run to another. Look through the list to make sure that all the information is to hand before starting.

1) LET BL = (your bank balance) / NEWLINE
2) DIM M (10) / NEWLINE
3) DIM N (10) / NEWLINE
4) DIM Q (10) / NEWLINE
5) LET D4 = (the day number) / NEWLINE
6) LET D5 = (the month number) / NEWLINE
7) LET D6 = (the last two digits in the year number) / NEWLINE

Key GO TO 200 and the main menu will appear. Select " C " to change the standing orders and then change them from zero and month zero to the amounts payable and the months when payment is due. The quarterly payments will only need one month number, not four.

Your program is now ready to run.

VARIABLES USED IN PERSONAL FINANCES

Cash handling system variables:

AJ	Adjusting amount of cash
A$	Signal
BL	Balance
D1	Day number
D2	Month number
D3	Year number, two digits only

Variables specific to Personal Finances:

B$	Another signal for use when A$ needs to stay set
D$	" MONTH DUE "
A	Any input that need not be permanent
C	Cheque book number
C1	Next cheque number
C2	Last cheque in book
C3	Next paying-in slip number
D4 to D6	To hold a second date
J and K	Loop counters
Z	Set to 100 000 as an arithmetic adjuster
Q, N and M	Arrays DIMensioned to (10) which hold the standing orders.

7 Banking

Having shown that the ZX81 is more than a match for personal finance problems we can now try it as a watchdog, keeping an eye on many accounts at once. At school we have a bank for the students. The bank is for the convenience of the users but it is felt to be important for educational reasons as well. Both the users and the student cashiers gain experience of an important aspect of modern life as they use and run the bank.

The bank attracts users from the lower school but many drift away as they move up the school. The initial enthusiasm needs something to sustain it once the novelty has worn off. Interest earned on the students' savings is the obvious way of retaining the customers, but too much of the organising teacher's time was being spent on the bank already. The prospect of having to calculate the interest due on an account every time a transaction occurred did not appeal. As soon as the ZX81 was seen to be offering useful services in other areas of the school, the bank staff became interested in computerising the bank. After some discussion a banking program was commissioned. The main objective was to allow the bank to offer interest. This was to be funded from the interest on the bank's assets held in a local High Street bank. After the program had been written and put to work, many other benefits arose. Daily accounts were printed automatically and so ceased to be an irritating chore which was sometimes put off until the next day. Monthly accounting and the printing of statements on all the accounts became the work of minutes rather than hours. The program became a great success which lifted student enthusiasm and revitalised the staff involvement which had sagged due to the extra burden which banking imposed on an already heavily committed teacher.

We were quite formal in the way that we attacked the program. The first thing we did was to sit down to some "system analysis". This was necessary to identify all the jobs that the computer could do. Developing the program would involve investing a lot of effort. It was important to make maximum use of this effort and not feel satisfied with sorting out the immediate problems. We were a little over enthusiastic at first because we thought it would be a good idea if the students were presented with a ledger page every time ten transactions were completed. We expected to run 200 accounts at first and so the machine would have to set aside enough space to store two hundred lots of ten transactions. With the most economical storage system we could devise this would have cost six thousand bytes. The final version of the program occupies roughly 5K of memory and takes about two minutes and forty-five seconds to load. The "load" time would have risen to around seven minutes if we were to print ledger pages and this time would have to be doubled to allow for the "save" time at the end of business. The bank is only open for half an hour a day! Having put off printing ledger pages until the machine can drive discs, we were left with these jobs to translate into basic.

OPENING THE BANK

i Print headings.

ii Request and store date.

iii Print float from last day's business, adjusted for any deposits at or

iv withdrawals from the main bank.

v Update the till.

vi Adjust all accounts for interest since the last day's business.

vii Print existing rate of interest and allow an opportunity to change it.

viii Start business with a well presented screen display.

TRANSACTIONS

ix Print a choice of operation.

x Request account number.

xi Print balance, request deposit or withdrawal and amount of money.

xii Check for negative balance, refuse withdrawals which would render an account overdrawn.

xiii Update balance and till.

To make sure that the float is kept to a minimum the bank requires notice of withdrawals over one pound and so:

xiv Store account number and amount of each notice of withdrawal.

xv Total and print out the amount needed from the main bank to cover the expected withdrawals.

ACCOUNTING

xvi Print total assets and liabilities (students' balances).

xvii Print balances on all accounts.

xviii Request interest due from the main bank.

xix Print final balance sheet.

OPENING AND CLOSING ACCOUNTS

xx Search for vacant accounts.

xxi Allocate new account to new member of the bank.

xxii Close accounts if the balance falls to zero.

Most of the writing was straightforward and was done at the machine. There were two areas which were a little too demanding for this and these were flow charted first. These jobs were: deciding on the number of days that had passed since the last day of business and deciding if a withdrawal was to be allowed; if it closed the account or if it was going to push the account into the red and so had to be refused.

The number of elapsed days was important; it was needed to calculate the interest since the last business. Because of the holidays, quite long periods could go by between business days and this had to be allowed for. What was needed was a way of deciding how many days there were in any month. Using "Thirty days hath September etc." and forgetting about leap years, we ended up with this solution:

D5 stores the month number and D7 stores the number of days in the month.

```
If D5 = 4 OR D5 = 6 OR D5 = 9 OR D5 = 11 THEN LET D7 = 30
```

4, 6, 9 and 11 represent April, June, September and November from the rhyme

```
If D5 = 2 THEN LET D7 = 28
```

takes care of February and, as "all the rest have thirty-one",

```
If D7 <> 30 AND D7 <> 28 THEN LET D7 = 31
```

Follow the logic of this section of program on the flow chart (Figure 7.1). If the month and year have not changed since last time it is only necessary to subtract the old day number from the new day number. When the month has changed the number of days in the old month has to be found. If more than one month has gone by, the number of days in each of them has to be added to a counter. The counter used is D8. At the end of this section D8 will contain: the remaining days in the old month, the number of days in each of the intervening months and the days that have passed so far in the new month.

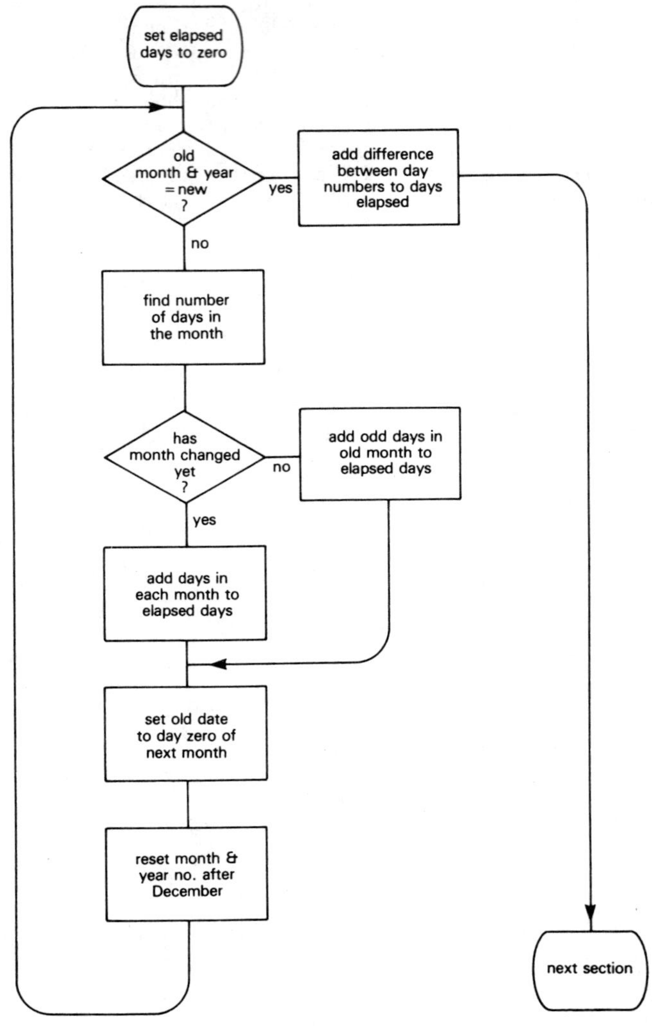

Figure 7.1 Deciding on days elapsed since last business

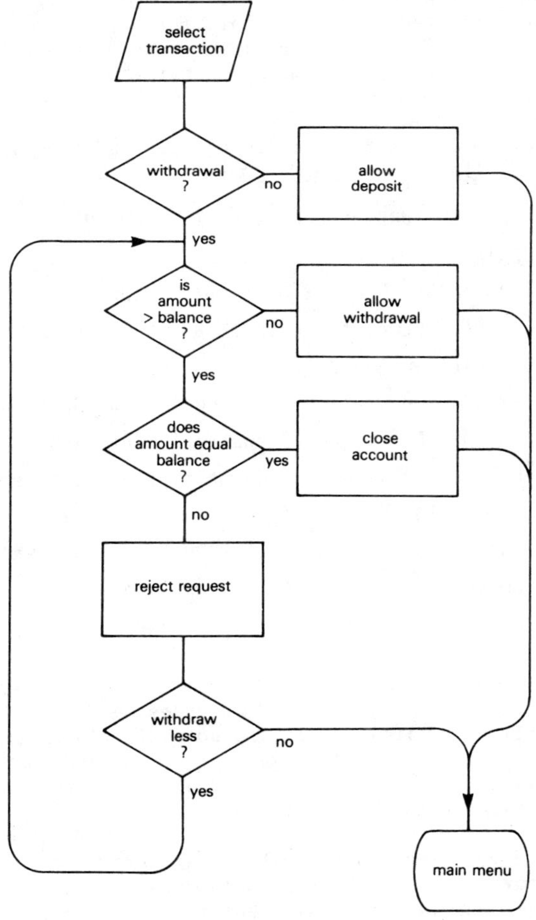

Figure 7.2 Coping with withdrawal requests

Deciding what to do about a withdrawal request involves asking a few more questions. If the request is for less than the balance in the account then there is no problem. The payment can be made. To avoid cluttering up the bank with a lot of accounts with less than a penny on deposit, a withdrawal which leaves less than 1p behind closes the account. The last possibility is that a student asks for more than is on deposit in his or her account. This must make the ZX81 print a refusal and give an opportunity for the request to be moderated. The flow chart for this section has no decision box for this last possibility because, if a request is for neither the exact balance nor less than the balance, it has to be for more.

Lines 1 to 199 of the program are occupied by the cash handling system which is listed on pages 60 to 72.

```
200    PRINT " THREADNEEDLE STREET SCHOOL BANK "
210    PRINT
220    PRINT D4 ; " / " ; D5 ; " / " ; D6
230    PRINT " FLOAT AT CLOSE OF BUSINESS WAS £ " ;
INT ( BL * 100 + .5 ) / 100
240    PRINT AT 8 , 0 ; " ANY DEPOSITS TO THE MAIN BANK? "
250    GO SUB 10              (input a sum of cash)
260    LET AS = AS + AJ       (add it to the ASsets store)
270    GO SUB 30              (deduct it from the float)
280    PRINT " ANY WITHDRAWALS FROM THE MAIN BANK? "
290    GO SUB 10              (input a sum of cash)
300    LET AS = AS - AJ
```

Later in the program we will be adding small fractions of a penny to the accounts and so printing the balances needs care. £5.6483929 will be a little confusing so it is tidied up a bit before printing. Line 230 multiplies by 100 and adds 0.5. Taking the integer value and dividing by 100 again gives the value £5.65, the original balance to the nearest penny.

The rest of this section is quite straightforward. D4, D5 and D6 are the stores for the day, month and year of the last day of business. BL is the variable which holds the bank's float, AS holds the assets on deposit at the main bank. AJ is changed every time the program goes to subroutine 10. The amount of money that will adjust the various balances is held in AJ. Subroutine 10 in the cash handling system allows the user to key in an amount. GO SUB 30 results in the adjusting amount being made negative and then added to the float. Withdrawals from the main bank have to be added to the float so the next line will be:

```
310    GO SUB 35
320    PRINT " FLOAT SHOULD BE £ " ; INT ( BL * 100 + .5 )
/ 100
330    PRINT
340    PRINT " IF THE RATE OF INTEREST HAS CHANGED FROM *
" ; R ; " * THEN KEY 1 , OTHERWISE KEY NEWLINE "
350    INPUT A$
360    IF A$ = " 1 " THEN GO SUB 600
370    CLS
380    GO SUB 60
```

You will have gathered that R is used to store the rate of interest. Very few variables are used in this program. The ones used are defined each time they appear for the first time but you will find a full list of variables, strings etc. at the end of the listing. At 600 there is a short subroutine which allows the rate of interest paid to be changed. Much use of subroutine 70 is made in this program because it is designed to be used by young, inexperienced operators. At 70, you will remember, is a routine which asks the user to check all data keyed in. For the same reason the number of keys that need to be pressed is very small. The numbers, the full stop, "M" and newline are the only ones. This means that a keyboard mask can be made with very few cutouts. Such a mask will avoid keying errors and will prevent the shift key being pressed. Much of the numerical input is fed into string A$ and treated as a single letter. This is to avoid the computer showing an error message if a letter is pressed when a figure is expected. The machine will accept letters and figures when it is told to input a string. The subroutine at 60 feeds a data into D1, D2 and D3. These three variables will hold the new date and, at the end of business, the new date will be fed into D4, D5 and D6 so that the computer will know the last date on which the bank was open when the program is loaded again.

The next section calculates the interest due on all accounts and does a lot of calculating which would take ages in slow mode, so the first instruction is:

```
400    FAST
410    LET D8 = 0
420    IF D5 = D2 AND D6 = D3 THEN GO TO 530
430    LET D7 = 0
```

```
440    IF D5 = 4 OR D5 = 6 OR D5 = 9 OR D5 = 11 THEN LET
D7 = 30
450    IF D5 = 2 THEN LET D7 = 28
460    IF D7 = 0 THEN LET D7 = 31
470    LET D8 = D8 + D7
475    LET D8 = D8 - D4
480    LET D5 = D5 + 1
490    LET D4 = 0
500    IF D5 > 12 THEN LET D6 = D6 + 1
510    IF D5 > 12 THEN LET D5 = D5 - 12
520    GO TO 420
```

D8 stores all the days that have passed since the bank was open. Line 420 checks to see if the month and the year has changed since last time. If they are the same then the next section will calculate D8. D7 is the store for the number of days in each month. Lines 440 to 460 decide on the number of days in the month. Line 460 is a little different from the line given earlier because we can use D7 as a signal that D7 has not been set. If it still equals 0 it has to be set to 31.

Line 475 is a cunning little check. The first time through the loop the day of the old date will be greater than 0 but a little later, at line 490, D4 is set to 0 for all subsequent trips through this section. On the first time through, the day number for the month is taken from the number of days in the month. This allows the twenty-one days between the 10th of January and the 1st of February to be added to the D8 store. All circuits after the first one have D4 set to zero so line 475 has no effect and the full number of days in the month is added. When the computer escapes from the loop the days in the new month are added to D8.

Lines 480 to 510 adjust the old date to bring it closer to the new date, allowing for year changes on the way.

```
530    LET D8 = D8 + D1 - D4
540    FOR J = 1 TO 200
550    IF A (J) < 10 THEN GO TO 570
560    LET A (J) = A (J) + A (J) * D8 * R / 36500
570    NEXT J
580    SLOW
590    GO TO 1000
```

Line 530 is a little more involved than it might appear. D4 may be the old day number but only if the computer has not gone around the loop in the previous section. If the loop was used then the value of D4 will have been set to zero. Lines 540 to 570 look at each account in turn. The accounts are stored in an array A dimensioned to 200. If the student has more than £9.99 then he or she is entitled to interest on the amount. The balance X the rate ÷ 100 × the number of days ÷ 365 = amount of interest. This is added to the balance. When the calculations are all finished the machine is set back into slow mode so that the rest of the display is smooth. At line 1000 the real business of the day starts but first there is a short input subroutine which allows the rate of interest to be changed.

```
600    CLS
610    PRINT " KEY THE NEW RATE OF INTEREST "
620    INPUT A
630    PRINT A ; " * PERCENT PER YEAR "
640    GO SUB 70
650    IF A$ <> " C " THEN GO TO 600
660    LET R = A
670    RETURN
```

Most of the sections start with a CLS statement to keep the screen clear and free from clutter. GO SUB 70 allows the input to be checked before it is allocated to R at line 660. The signal, A$ <> "C", causes the value of A to be overwritten by sending the machine back to line 600.

And now down to business.

```
1000   CLS
1010   PRINT " THREADNEEDLE STREET SCHOOL BANK "
(this may be printed in inverse graphics)
1020   PRINT AT 5 , 0 ; " SELECT OPERATION "
1030   PRINT
1040   PRINT " TRANSACTION  KEY 1 "
1050   PRINT " WITHDRAWAL NOTICE  KEY 2 "
1060   PRINT " END OF BUSINESS  KEY 3 "
1070   PRINT " MONTHLY ACCOUNTS  KEY 4 "
1080   PRINT " TO OPEN NEW ACCOUNT  KEY 5 "
1100   INPUT A$
```

```
1110    IF A$ = " 1 " THEN GO TO 1500
1120    IF A$ = " 2 " THEN GO TO 3000
1130    IF A$ = " 3 " THEN GO TO 4000
1140    IF A$ = " 4 " THEN GO TO 5000
1150    IF A$ = " 5 " THEN GO TO 5500
```

The menu always looks better for a little thought in laying it out. The spaces cost a few bytes and the five lines of spacing cost a few more. Perhaps the inverse graphs are a little trouble to produce on the ZX81 but, this display will be on the screen for most of the time, and the more professional it looks the more confidence it may inspire in the bank users. If the input at 1100 is incorrect the control of the computer will move to line 1160. This line sends the machine to an "I don't understand" section a little later on.

```
1160    GO SUB 1175
1170    GO TO 1000
1175    CLS
1180    PRINT AT 10, 0 ; " SORRY, I DONT UNDERSTAND "
1190    PRINT " KEY AGAIN "
1200    FOR J = 1 TO 250
1210    NEXT J
1220    RETURN
```

The "sorry, I dont understand" bit looks good in inverse graphics in the middle of the screen. The seemingly useless FOR/NEXT loop is a way of generating a delay before sending the machine back to the menu. The pause function causes some picture flicker and this counting up to 250 in slow mode approach is a lot smoother. The delay is just enough to allow the message to be read comfortably.

Now the transactions can begin.

```
1500    CLS
1510    PRINT " KEY ACCOUNT NO. "
1520    INPUT N
1530    PRINT AT 5 , 0 ; " ACCOUNT * " ; N
1540    GO SUB 70
1550    IF A$ <> " C " THEN GO TO 1500
1555    CLS
```

```
1560   IF A (N) < 0 THEN PRINT " OVERDRAWN BY £ " ; INT ( A
(N) * 100 + .5) / 100
1570   IF A (N) >= 0 THEN PRINT " £ " ; INT ( A (N) * 100 +
.5 ) / 100 ; " * IN CREDIT "
1580   PRINT " WITHDRAWAL  KEY 1 "
1590   PRINT " DEPOSIT  KEY 2 "
1600   INPUT M
```

Here again, the input is checked for accuracy every time it is keyed in.

As with the personal finances program, it is necessary to make the display of credit balances different from the display of overdrafts. There should never be any account which is overdrawn but the staff might start using the bank and might use silver tongued charm to obtain an overdraft. The interest calculator works just as well at charging interest on overdrawn accounts as it does augmenting credit balances.

```
1610   IF M <> 1 AND M <> 2 THEN GO SUB 1175
1620   IF M <> 1 AND M <> 2 THEN GO TO 1560
1625   CLS
1630   IF M = 1 THEN PRINT " WITHDRAWAL "
1640   IF M = 2 THEN PRINT " DEPOSIT "
1650   GO SUB 10
```

More input checks, the routine at 1175 is the "I don't understand" one. Line 1650 asks for the amount of the withdrawal or deposit and then follows a series of questions that the computer asks itself. These are of the form:

> Is the signal anything other than the one appropriate to the next section? If so bypass the next section.

There is a question of this type at line 1700, 1770 and 1850.

```
1700   IF M = 1 THEN GO TO 1770  (ie. bypass this section)
1710   LET A(N) = A(N) + AJ      (add the amount to balance)
1720   GO SUB 35                 (add the amount to float)
1730   PRINT " BALANCE NOW STANDS AT £ "; INT ( A (N) *
100 + .5)/ 100
```

```
1740    PRINT " KEY N/L "    (N/L for newline to save space)
1750    INPUT A$             (pause til ready)
1760    GO TO 1000           (back to menu)
```

That part of the program allowed any deposit to proceed, increased the float and the individual balance by the amount of the deposit, and then returned to the menu for the next transaction. The situation with withdrawals is more complex, as was seen when we were considering the flow diagram.

```
1770    IF AJ >= INT ( A (N) * 100 + .5 ) / 100 THEN GO TO
1850
```

Which means, if the amount is less than the balance in the account then do this bit, otherwise go to the next section.

```
1780    LET A (N) = A (N) - AJ    (deduct amount from balance)
1790    GO SUB 30                 (deduct from float)
1800    PRINT " BALANCE NOW STANDS AT £ " ; INT ( A(N) *
100 + .5 ) / 100
1810    PRINT " KEY N/L "
1820    INPUT A$                  (signal when ready)
1830    GO TO 1000                (return to menu)
```

And now another of those questions:

```
1850    IF AJ <> INT ( A(N) * 100 + .5 ) / 100 THEN GO TO
2000
```

Which means, if the amount is the same as the balance and so the account is being closed then do this bit, otherwise go to the next section.

```
1860    CLS
1870    PRINT " THIS WITHDRAWAL CLOSES THE ACCOUNT "
1880    GO SUB 70                 (check for mistake)
1890    IF A$ <> " C " THEN GO TO 1000    (back to menu if
                                            mistake)
1900    PRINT " ACCOUNT * " ; N ; " * CLOSED BY A PAYMENT OF
£ " ; INT ( A (N) * 100 + .5 ) / 100
1910    LET A (N) = 0             (closes a/c)
```

```
1920    GO SUB 30                  (deducts amount from float)
1930    PRINT " KEY N/L "
1940    INPUT A$                   (signal when ready)
1950    GO TO 1000                 (return to menu)
```

The account has to be set to zero at line 1910 when it is closed because there is a search section later which looks for spare account numbers for new customers and recognises them only because they are completely empty and don't contain the odd 1/10000 of a penny.

And now the part that all bankers like; refusing payment. No need for a question this time. If all the other questions were inappropriate then the amount required must be more than the balance. This section is only reached in this circumstance because all the other sections return the machine to the menu.

```
2000    CLS
2010    PRINT " NOT ENOUGH IN ACCOUNT "  (inverse graphics
                                          will have to do
                                          instead of red!)
2020    PRINT " KEY N/L "
2030    INPUT A$                         (signal when ready)
2040    GO TO 1000
```

This next part of the code is called when the cashier keys "2" in response to the menu. It records all withdrawal notices, the account number and the amount required. At the end of the day the total required to meet the needs of the next day's withdrawals is printed so that the cash can be drawn from the main bank. The amount of cash can be kept to a minimum in this way but there should always be enough for all withdrawals. When students are handling money it is always as well to avoid having excessive sums hanging around. Losses and miscalculations can be kept to a minimum in this way.

```
3000    CLS
3010    PRINT " KEY ACCOUNT NO. "
3020    INPUT N
3030    PRINT " KEY AMOUNT NEEDED "
3040    INPUT M
3050    LPRINT " £ " ; M ; " * REQUIRED FOR ACCOUNT NO. * "
; N
```

```
3060   LET W = W + M
3080   GO TO 1000                (return to menu)
```

W stores the total cash required for the next day's withdrawals. The command LPRINT appears here for the first time. This is the first of the commands which cause the printer to record information on paper. All requests for withdrawals will be recorded on the daily statement as a result of line 3050. At the end of business the total of all these requests, stored in variable "W", will be printed out. "W" will be set to zero in preparation for the next day of business, before the data is stored on tape. A few other adjustments are needed at this stage. The float must be printed out for checking, and the old date has to be changed to the present date. Keying "3" at the menu starts the computer working at:

```
4000   CLS
4010   PRINT " END OF BUSINESS STATEMENT FOR " , D1 ; " / "
; D2 ; " / " ; D3
4020   LET D4 = D1
4030   LET D5 = D2
4040   LET D6 = D3
4050   PRINT
4060   PRINT " TOTAL REQUIRED FOR WITHDRAWALS £ " ; W
4070   PRINT
4080   PRINT " FLOAT SHOULD CONTAIN £ " ; INT ( BL * 100 +
.5 ) / 100
4090   COPY
4100   PRINT " KEY N/L "
4110   INPUT A$
4120   GO TO 6000
```

In this section there is the first use of the printer command " COPY " which makes the printer copy the screen display onto paper. If there is no printer available then these printer commands will have to be replaced by INPUT A$ commands to allow the information to be printed on the screen and then copied by hand. Keying NEWLINE will then allow the program to continue.

Lines 5000 to 5400 print out the monthly accounts. The state of all the balances are printed using printer command "COPY" and the balance sheet is displayed and printed in the same way.

```
5000   CLS
5010   PRINT " THREADNEEDLE STREET SCHOOL BANK "
5020   PRINT
5030   PRINT " MONTHLY ACCOUNTS AS AT * " ; D1 ; " / " ;
D2 ; " / " ; D3
5040   PRINT
5050   PRINT " KEY ANY INTEREST RECEIVED FROM THE MAIN BANK '
5060   COPY
5070   GO SUB 10
5080   LET AS = AS + AJ
5090   CLS
5100   PRINT " £ " ; AJ
5110   PRINT " TOTAL ASSETS HELD "
5120   PRINT " £ " ; INT ( AS * 100 + .5 ) / 100; " * ON
DEPOSIT AT BANK "
5130   PRINT " £ " ; INT ( BL * 100 + .5 ) / 100; " * HELD
IN TILL "
5135   PRINT " __________ "
5140   PRINT " £ " ; INT ( BL * 100 + .5 ) / 100 + INT
( AS * 100 + .5 ) / 100 ; " * TOTAL "
5150   COPY
```

Lines 5120 and 5130 print the two forms of the bank's assets. 5135 makes the previous two lines into an addition sum to which line 5140 is the answer. The screen was cleared at line 5000 so the copy command will result in a well headed, neatly laid out start to the balance sheet. This will be followed by a statement of the state of each account which will occupy one hundred lines. A screenful or slightly less will be allowed to build up. This will be copied by the printer and then cleared for another screenful. The table will be constructed using the TAB statement.

```
5200   CLS
5210   PRINT " TOTAL LIABILITIES"
5220   PRINT
5230   PRINT " A/C " ; TAB 8 ; " BAL " ; TAB 16 ; " A/C " ;
TAB 24 ; " BAL "
```

```
5240    LET LI = 0
5250    LET K = 0
5260    FOR J = 1 TO 200     (to count through the a/cs)
5270    PRINT J ; TAB 8 ; INT ( A (J) * 100 + .5 ) / 100;
5280    LET LI = LI + A(J)   (LI is the liabilities store)
5290    LET J = J + 1        (for the 2nd half of the line)
5300    PRINT ; TAB 16 ; J ; TAB 24; INT ( A(J) * 100 + .5 )
/ 100
5310    LET LI = LI + A(J)
5320    LET K = K + 1
5330    IF K = 18 THEN COPY   (prints 18 lines at a time)
5340    IF K = 18 THEN CLS    (makes way for 18 more)
5350    IF K = 18 THEN LET K = 0 (clears K for the next count
5360    NEXT J
5370    PRINT                 (space to improve layout)
5380    PRINT " TOTAL LIABILITIES = £ " ; INT ( LI * 100 +
.5 ) / 100
5390    COPY
5400    GO TO 1000
```

Watch out for some important details in this section. There is a semicolon at the end of line 5270 but not at the end of the similar line, 5300. The variable which holds the total on deposit at the school bank is " LI " for LIabilities and not " L one ".

The final part of the program contains a search for empty accounts and the auto restart routine. The search is selected by keying "5" at the menu.

```
5500    CLS
5505    LET X = 1            (X will count through the a/cs)
5510    IF A(X) = 0 THEN PRINT " ACCOUNT NO. * " ; X ;
" * IS FREE "
5520    IF A(X) = 0 THEN GO TO 5550   (escape from loop)
5530    LET X = X + 1                 (next account)
5535    IF X = 201 THEN PRINT " NO VACANT ACCOUNTS "
5540    IF X = 201 THEN GO TO 5550
```

```
5545   GO TO 5510      (goes round again)
5550   PRINT " KEY NEWLINE "
5560   INPUT A$        (signal when ready)
5570   GO TO 1000      (return to menu)
```

And finally, the auto start:

```
6000   LET W = 0       (sets withdrawal requests to zero)
6010   CLS
6020   PRINT AT 10, 10; " START TAPE "
6030   PRINT TAB 10; " KEY NEWLINE "
6040   INPUT A$
6050   CLS
6060   SAVE " BANK "
6070   GO TO 200
```

VARIABLES, SUBROUTINES AND ARRAYS USED IN THE BANKING PROGRAM

Subroutines (cash handling system)	Input a sum of cash	10 - 29
	Render a sum negative	30 - 33
	Add to float	35 - 42
	Input the date	60 - 66
	Check for and signal mistakes	70 - 75
(specific to the bank program)	Change rate of interest	600 - 670
	Signal typing error	1175 - 1220

Arrays A(200) storage for up to 200 accounts

String A$ signal string

Variables

BL	Float
AJ	Adjusting sum of cash
D1,2,3	New date
D4,5,6	Old date
D7	Number of days in each month
D8	Total days since last business
AS	Bank's assets at the main bank
R	Rate of interest being offered to students
W	Amount needed for withdrawal requests
LI	Total liabilities (sum of all balances)
J,X,K	Various counters

As it stands the program will crash the first time it is used! Don't worry though, there is a reason. In the personal finances program there was a long section of code which allowed the user to set up the system with all the information on cheque numbers, standing orders etc. This section was used once and then deleted. To avoid all that wasted keying in and then deleting, no such section has been written into this program. Follow these instructions to set up the system. The commands are keyed in without line numbers so that, when NEWLINE is keyed, the command is executed immediately. It would be wise to read through the list of commands to make sure that all the information needed is to hand.

```
DIM A ( 200 )          (or as many accounts as may be opened)
NEWLINE
LET BL = ( amount of cash in till )
NEWLINE
LET D4 = ( day number )
NEWLINE
LET D5 = ( month number )
NEWLINE
LET D6 = ( year number, last two digits )
NEWLINE
LET AS = ( total cash on deposit at the main bank )
NEWLINE
LET R = ( rate of interest )
NEWLINE
```

The method of calculating interest gives an approximation to compound interest. The more days the bank is open each year, the closer the approximation. The rate offered should be kept significantly lower than the rate given by the main bank to allow a little profit to cover expenses.

After this setting up procedure, the bank is ready for computerised business.

The cutout in the following figure, made from stiff card or plastic sheet, will prevent the majority of crashes due to inappropriate input. An extra cutout for the SHIFT key will make the "rubout" facility available but the typing error routine should make this unnecessary.

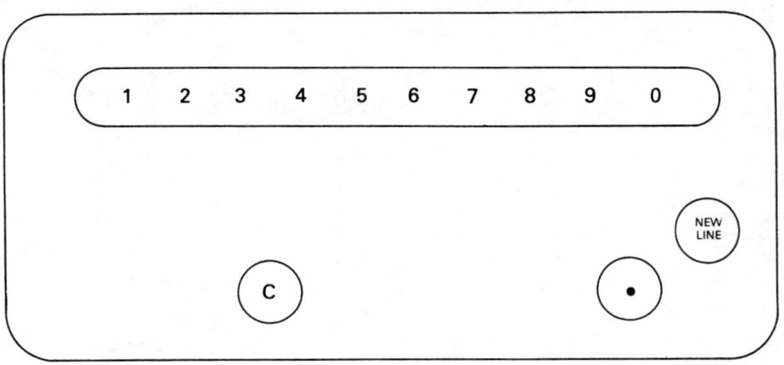

Figure 7.3 Keyboard cutout for use with the School Bank Program

8 Bulk Storage

Critics are quick to point out that the ZX81 is just a toy. They tell us that it will never do any serious data processing because it has two serious limitations. It cannot be expanded beyond 16K of random access memory and it cannot handle data files. Now that RAM packs of 64K and more have been developed, the first objection can be settled simply by paying out for extra RAM.

But it must be said that the critics do have a point. With the standard 16K RAM pack the storage space is limited and anything that is stored must fit into whatever space is left after the program has been loaded. How much can be stored? Each number held by the machine takes up five bytes and so the fully expanded ZX81 will hold 3276 numbers, but this leaves no space for the program which is needed to get the numbers into the machine in the first place. The program described in this chapter occupies 4½K so there remains space for only 2350 numbers All this assumes that conventional methods of storage are used. Over two thousand pieces of information is quite a lot but the adoption of some unorthodox methods allows very much more to be stored. The numbers are not only stored but can be retrieved from the files under which they are held, in a number of interesting ways that allow correlations to be determined. The retrieval criteria can be specified from the keyboard while the program is running, so interesting patterns that emerge can be investigated further by subtly changing the search criteria.

The program was originally written for the ZX80 as a fun program which ran a mythical rabbit farm and organised the breeding to ensure maximum success at the National Bunny Show. The storage system used was very similar to the system used here, but the technique used to sort out the information was rather clumsy. The rabbit program was written to show off just what the earlier computer could do with a little acrobatic BASIC. It did that job well but the method used to extract the information prevented development of the program for more serious work. The advent of the ZX81 re-awakened my interest in the storage technique. The new computer had " string slicing " and some other useful string handling facilities which could solve the data extraction difficulties. The basic idea was soon worked up into a much more elegant and potentially useful program. The program which is described later is in regular use, doing serious data processing.

SOLVING THE STORAGE PROBLEM

The ZX81 can hold some very large numbers indeed. The largest that can be stored with absolute accuracy, however, is an eight digit number. If nine digit numbers are entered, there is a risk that the last digit will be changed slightly as the computer moves it around inside the memory. Limiting ourselves to eight digit numbers will ensure that any information fed into the machine is not corrupted. Now that the maximum size of numbers has been set we can look at ways of storing information in these numbers. If the information to be stored can be represented by ten symbols, then the symbols 0 to 9 can be used. Adult shoe sizes are easy to represent in this way. Few people have feet larger than size 11 or smaller than size 3. By subtracting 2 from a person's shoe size, the information can be stored in a one digit number. So why worry about eight digit numbers? Well, eight pieces of information can be stored in an eight digit number as long as they can be represented by the symbols, 0 to 9.

The rabbit program used the ZX80's five digit numbers as follows:

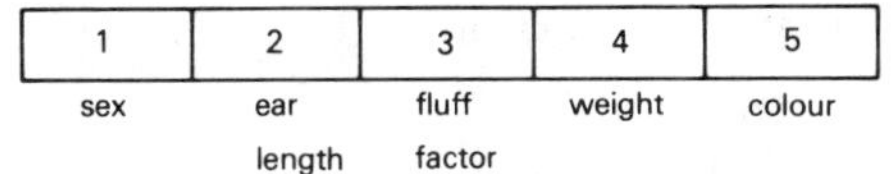

The first digit was used for the sex of the rabbit because the maximum that could be stored was 32767, and if sex was represented by 1 for male and 2 for female, then the largest number to be accommodated was 29999, well inside the limit. Ear length could be from 0 to 9 cm or these digits could represent lengths between 5 and 14 cm. The decoding of the information was a simple matter. It was necessary to include checks on the input though. If 10 was entered for the ear length by mistake, then the rabbit would be described by the computer as having no ears at all and as being a little over weight. The ear information would have spilled over into the space set aside for storing the weight code. The following check prevented such mishaps:

```
100     PRINT " KEY THE EAR LENGTH "
110     INPUT A
120     IF A < 0 OR A > 9 THEN GO TO 1000
```

and at line 1000 could be a few lines which explain the mistake, clear the screen and return the user to the input section.

Fluff factor, colour etc. were all represented by the symbols 0 to 9 and fed into the stores by a process of multiplication by ten, followed by addition. To store the colour "6" in the final digit of a number, all that was needed was:

```
10      PRINT " KEY COLOUR "
20      INPUT A
30      (check routine)
40      LET X = A
```

which leaves the variable X containing 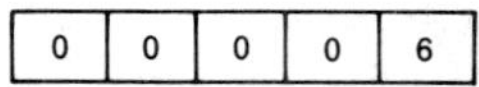

To store the weight "9" in the fourth digit:

```
50      PRINT " KEY WEIGHT IN RABBIT UNITS "
60      INPUT A
70      (check routine)
80      LET X = X + A * 10
```

which leaves the variable X containing

0	0	0	9	6

The fluff code was multiplied by 100 before storing, the ear length by 1000 and the sex by 10000.

Eventually, X might hold

1	1	8	9	6

which represents an extraordinarily fluffy buck rabbit with very short ears, a cream coat and a weight problem.

Disentangling the information was more difficult. The ZX80's integer arithmetic was useful in isolating the digits. If the fluff factor stored in digit three had to be printed then the following method had to be used:

X was divided by 100 and the result was stored in A

11896 / 100 = 118 in integer arithmetic so A = 118

X was next divided by 1000 and the result was stored in B

11896 / 1000 = 11 in integer arithmetic so B = 11

B was multiplied by 10 and the result was stored in C

11 * 10 = 110 so C = 110

The fluff factor was found by taking C from A

118 - 110 = 8

The method worked but the code was intricate to say the least. Doe number six needed a mate who would match her qualities and help her produce a prize winning litter. This is the line which found him:

```
430    IF A ( L * 3 - 1 ) / 100 = 117 AND A ( L * 3 ) / 1000
< 19 AND A ( L * 3 ) / 1000 > 15 AND A ( L * 3 ) / 100 -
( A ( L * 3 ) / 1000 ) * 10 > 5 AND ( A ( L * 3 ) / 100 ) -
( A ( L * 3 ) / 1000 ) * 10 < 9 THEN PRINT A ( L * 3 - 2 ) ,
```

The new machine decodes the stored data much more neatly. Each eight digit number is turned into a string of eight characters by using the STR$ facility. This string of characters can be sliced up using the string slicing function to isolate any required group of characters. The group of characters is next converted into a number using the VAL function.

Suppose X contains the value 79218161.

```
100    LET A$ = STR$  X
```

will give a string of characters "79218161".

```
110    PRINT A$  ( 2 TO 4 )
```

will give "921" while:

```
110    PRINT A$  ( 5 TO 5 )
```

will result in "8" being printed on the screen.

The string of characters is turned back into a number again by:

```
200    LET B = VAL A$  ( 5 TO 5 )
```

which sets B equal to 8.

Now that the logical basis of the program has been explained we can start work on the program itself. Each item is described by sixteen different factors. The items could be anything but, for the purposes of this chapter they will be imaginary engineering artefacts with sixteen different characteristics. To make the program realistic, different ranges of symbols are used to describe these characteristics, because it is unlikely that all the useful information can be adequately represented by the symbols 0 to 9. The range of symbols used is:

0 to 9   0 to 99   0 to 999

and the following chart gives the characteristics, the range of values for each and the number of digits needed to store these values.

	Characteristic	Range of values	Digits used
1	area	0 - 9	1
2	bore	0 - 58	2
3	capacity	0 - 90	2
4	depth	0 - 115	3
5	end size	0 - 15	2
6	finish	0 - 27	2
7	gromet size	0 - 10	2
8	height	60 - 65	1
9	internal ribbing	2 or 4	1
10	joist stress	0 - 9	1
11	kink resistance	0 - 700	3
12	length	0 - 500	3
13	mass	0 - 95	2
14	modular frequency	0 - 99	2
15	outside diameter	0 - 20	2
16	pressure	5 - 10	1

There are thirty digits used for the storage of this information and there are only eight in the largest number that can be stored safely. Four of these eight digit numbers can hold thirty-two digits and so four arrays of numbers will have to be set up to hold all the information. The information is stored in these arrays in the following way:

Storage in the Arrays

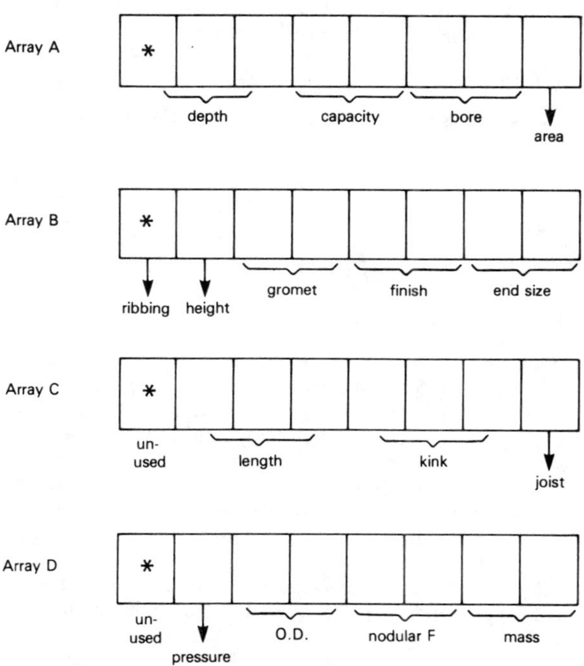

Figure 8.5 Storage in the arrays

* this digit must always contain a value other than zero to ensure that the string that is generated by STR$ is eight characters long. There is a safeguard in the program to make sure this is always so.

When the four main arrays are being set up, a fifth is organised to hold the information which is eventually extracted from the stored data. This array will have exactly the same number of elements to make the transfer of data efficient.

SUBROUTINES TO CHECK THE INPUT

The number of routines that you decide to include will depend on the experience of the user of the program. The first routine to be described is essential because even the most experienced typist makes mistakes and this routine allows any mistakes to be corrected before the information is finally accepted. The routine is called four times in the input loop so that only a few data will have to be repeated if a mistake is made.

```
1      GO TO 2000
2      PRINT " KEY C IF THESE ARE OK, OTHERWISE KEY NEWLINE "
3      INPUT A$
4      CLS
5      PRINT " ITEM NO. * " ; J
6      PRINT
7      RETURN
```

Line 1 by-passes the subroutines. This line will probably not be necessary because it is unlikely that the command RUN will ever be used to start this program off but it is better to be on the safe side. Line 5 prints up the heading again after the screen has been cleared. It is surprising how often you forget which item is being described, half way through an input loop. Keying "NEWLINE" alone will cause the machine to ask for all the information again, and the fresh data will be subject to the same check procedure.

The next subroutines are for inexperienced users, those who might enter a letter in place of a number, or who might key in information with too many digits which will spill over into space set aside for other data. If there is the slightest risk that this sort of problem will happen, then it is worth the trouble to key in the extra lines. The more checks that are included the more crashproof the program will be. The cost of this benefit is that the LOAD/SAVE time will be increased and the storage space will be reduced. There are three of these routines, for one to three digit data. If you decide to include these then the input lines given later will have to be " INPUT A$ " rather than " INPUT A ". String input will accept a letter or a number but has to be turned into a numerical value by the use of VAL before it can be used in the main part of the loop.

```
10     LET A = D
11     IF VAL A$ < 0 OR VAL A$ > 9 THEN RETURN
12     GO TO 18
```

```
13      LET A = D
14      IF VAL A$ < 0 OR VAL A$ > 99 THEN RETURN
15      GO TO 18
16      LET A = D
17      IF VAL A$ < 0 OR VAL A$ > 999 THEN RETURN
18      LET A = VAL A$
19      RETURN
```

In the main loop, if A has the value 1000 then the machine will know that an error has been made in the input and the data will be rejected. The appropriate routine will have to be selected according to the number of digits in the data and the address of the GO SUB line programmed accordingly.

A great deal of code now follows. It is most unlikely that any user will have a task which fits this storage system exactly but the system is given in full, nevertheless, because it illustrates the different types of storage and the use of the optional check routines. The adaption of the storage loop to suit the users information will take careful planning, but should present no real difficulty. The code is lengthy but quite straightforward, so it is given in one large chunk.

```
100     FOR J = 1 TO Z         (Z will be set to the number of
                                items)
110     GO SUB 4               (a cheap way of printing the
                                item number)
120     PRINT " KEY AREA " ,    (comma to cause the value to
                                 print on the same line)
130     INPUT A    (or A$ if check routine is to be used)
132     GO SUB 10
134     IF A = D THEN PRINT " ERROR "
136     IF A = D THEN GO TO 280
140     LET A ( J ) = A
150     PRINT A
160     PRINT " KEY BORE " ,
170     INPUT A    (or A$ if check routine is to be used)
172/6   GO SUB 13 and then the rest of the routine
180     LET A ( J ) = A ( J ) + A * B  (B is set to 10 later)
190     PRINT A
```

```
200     PRINT " KEY CAPACITY " ,
210     INPUT A ( or A$ )
212/6   GO SUB 13 etc.
220     LET A ( J ) = A ( J ) + A * D  (D is set to 1000
                                         later)

230     PRINT A
240     PRINT " KEY DEPTH " ,
250     INPUT A ( or A$ )
252/6   GO SUB 16 etc.
260     LET A ( J ) = A ( J ) + A * F + H
270     PRINT A
```

It could be that the depth of this particular item is zero. If so the eighth digit will be empty and when the array element is turned into a string there will be less than eight characters in it. The careful management of the string slicing will be spoilt and the output will be false. H is added to the array element to prevent this from happening.

10 000 000 will have to be subtracted from the element some way or other later on but more of that when we come to it. The use of H here reduces the capacity of the final digit to 8. It might be considered necessary to write three more subroutines to check for information between the ranges 0 - 8, 0 - 98 and 0 - 998. Once you start writing routines to protect the machine from inappropriate data, the amount of code needed to protect the program completely becomes a little extravagant. Now that the information to fill the element from the first array is in, it is time to call the first subroutine and allow the data to be dumped.

```
280     GO SUB 2
290     IF A$ <> " C " THEN GO TO 120
```

And now we can go on to fill up the elements of array B.

```
300     PRINT " KEY END SIZE " ,
310     INPUT A ( or A$ )
312/6   GO SUB 13 etc.
320     LET B ( J ) = A
330     PRINT A
340     PRINT " FINISH " ,
350     INPUT A ( or A$ )
```

```
352/6  GO SUB 13 etc.
360    LET B ( J ) = B ( J ) + A * C
370    PRINT A
380    PRINT " KEY GROMET SIZE " ,
390    INPUT A ( or A$ )
392/6  GO SUB 13 etc.
400    LET B ( J ) = B ( J ) + A * E
410    PRINT A
420    PRINT " HEIGHT " ,
430    INPUT A ( or A$ )
432/6  GO SUB 10 etc.
440    LET B ( J ) = B ( J ) + A * G
450    PRINT A
460    PRINT " RIBBING " ,
470    INPUT A ( or A$ )
472/6  GO SUB 10 etc. or even the 0 to 8 routines because
H crops up again in the next line
480    LET B ( J ) = B ( J ) + A * H + H
490    PRINT A
```

It is now time to call the first subroutine again:

```
500    GO SUB 2
505    IF A$ <> " C " THEN GO TO 300
```

And on to fill up array C:

```
510    PRINT " KEY JOIST STRESS " ,
520    INPUT A ( or A$ )
522/6  GO SUB 10 etc.
530    LET C ( J ) = A
540    PRINT A
550    PRINT " KEY KINK RESISTANCE " ,
560    INPUT A ( or A$ )
562/6  GO SUB 16 etc.
570    LET C ( J ) = C ( J ) + A * B
```

```
580     PRINT A
590     PRINT " KEY LENGTH " ,
600     INPUT A ( or A$ )
602/6   GO SUB 16 etc.
610     LET C ( J ) = C ( J ) + A * E + H  (H to fill the
                                             element)
620     PRINT A
630     REM SPARE DIGIT   (next lines left for possible
                           later use)

670     GO SUB 2
680     IF A$ <> " C " THEN GO TO 510
```

And now the final array element can be filled. As with the previous one, this element has a digit which is not used and there is a REM statement, which indicates where the spare space is for future reference. The data describing this item is now all in, so it is unnecessary to print the heading that was needed after each of the other checks. Subroutine 2 is not called this time, a shortened version is added to the program at this stage. Lines 850 to 880 do the checking. Just before the end of the loop there is a section, between lines 890 and 940, which allows the user to select any article for description. It is not necessary to accept the next one that the computer suggests.

```
690     PRINT " KEY MASS " ,
700     INPUT A ( or A$ )
702/6   GO SUB 13 etc.
710     LET D ( J ) = A
720     PRINT A
730     PRINT " NODULAR FREQUENCY " ,
740     INPUT A ( or A$ )
742/6   GO SUB 13 etc.
750     LET D ( J ) = D ( J ) + A * C
760     PRINT A
770     PRINT " KEY OUTSIDE DIAM. " ,
780     INPUT A
782/6   GO SUB 13 etc.
790     LET D ( J ) = D ( J ) + A * E
800     PRINT A
```

```
810     PRINT " KEY PRESSURE " ,
820     INPUT A ( or A$ )
822/6   GO SUB 10 etc.
830     LET D ( J ) = D ( J ) + A * G + H  (to fill the
                                             element)
840     PRINT A
845     REM SPARE DIGIT
850     PRINT " KEY C IF THESE ARE OK OTHERWISE NEWLINE "
860     INPUT A$
870     CLS
880     IF A$ <> " C " THEN GO TO 690
```

And the next section allows the choice of any item for treatment next. To stop entering data, all that is needed is to enter a number greater than the total number of items. This sets J equal to more than the limit set in the FOR statement, so the machine moves on to the next section.

```
890     PRINT AT B , 0 ; " ITEM * " ; J ; " * ENTERED "
900     PRINT
910     PRINT " KEY Ø TO ENTER NEXT ITEM "
920     PRINT " KEY THE NUMBER FOR ANOTHER ITEM "
930     INPUT A
940     IF A <> Ø THEN LET J = A - 1
950     NEXT J
960     CLS
970     GO TO 2000
```

When all the information is in, lines 960 and 970 clear the screen and send the computer off to a menu which allows the information to be sorted. The next section to be given is another menu, this time one which allows the user tc select one of the ways in which the items are described.

```
1000    PRINT " INITIAL SEARCH "
1010    PRINT " TO SPECIFY " , " KEY "
1011    PRINT " AREA " , 0
1012    PRINT " BORE " , 1
1013    PRINT " CAPACITY " , 2
1014    PRINT " DEPTH " , 3
```

```
1015   PRINT " END SIZE " , 4
1016   PRINT " FINISH " , 5
1017   PRINT " GROMET SIZE " , 6
1018   PRINT " HEIGHT " , 7
1019   PRINT " INTERNAL RIBBING " , 8
1020   PRINT " JOIST STRESS " , 9
1021   PRINT " KINK RESISTANCE " , 10
1022   PRINT " LENGTH " , 11
1023   PRINT " MASS " , 12
1024   PRINT " NODULAR FREQUENCY " , 13
1025   PRINT " OUTER DIAM. " , 14
1026   PRINT " PRESSURE " , 15
```

Section which allows a selection to be made from the menu:

```
1030   INPUT A$
1035   CLS
1040   LET A = VAL A$
1050   IF A < 0 OR A > 15 THEN GO TO 1000
```

Having made a choice the user is next requested to specify the range of values he or she is interested in finding.

```
1100   PRINT " RANGE OF SEARCH "
1110   PRINT
1120   PRINT " KEY MINIMUM " ,
1130   INPUT A$
1140   LET L = VAL A$
1150   PRINT L
1160   PRINT " KEY MAXIMUM " ,
1170   INPUT A$
1180   LET M = VAL A$
1190   PRINT M
1200   PRINT
1210   PRINT " KEY C IF CORRECT OTHERWISE NEWLINE "
1220   INPUT A$
```

```
1230    CLS
1240    IF A$ <> " C " THEN GO TO 1100
```

The first search is now set up but the computer does not yet know where the information is held or how many digits it needs to extract from the stored numbers. The code which follows produces no screen output and needs to be worked through as quickly as possible, so the first command is to put the computer into fast mode. When setting up a system of your own, you will have to work out the values of X and Y in the section which follows. These two variables are set to the digit numbers of the array elements where the relevant information is held.

```
1300    FAST
1301    IF A = 0 OR A = 9 THEN LET X = 8
1305    IF A = 0 OR A = 9 THEN LET Y = 8
1310    IF A = 1 THEN LET X = 6
1315    IF A = 1 THEN LET Y = 7
1320    IF A = 2 THEN LET X = 4
1325    IF A = 2 THEN LET Y = 5
1330    IF A = 3 THEN LET X = 1
1335    IF A = 3 THEN LET Y = 3
1340    IF A = 4 OR A = 12 THEN LET X = 7
1345    IF A = 4 OR A = 12 THEN LET Y = 8
1350    IF A = 5 OR A = 13 THEN LET X = 5
1355    IF A = 5 OR A = 13 THEN LET Y = 6
1360    IF A = 6 OR A = 14 THEN LET X = 3
1365    IF A = 6 OR A = 14 THEN LET Y = 4
1370    IF A = 7 OR A = 15 THEN LET X = 2
1375    IF A = 7 OR A = 15 THEN LET Y = 2
1380    IF A = 8 THEN LET X = 1
1385    IF A = 8 THEN LET Y = 1
1390    IF A = 10 THEN LET X = 5
1395    IF A = 10 THEN LET Y = 7
1400    IF A = 11 THEN LET X = 2
1405    IF A = 11 THEN LET Y = 4
1410    SLOW
1420    RETURN
```

Line 1420 betrays the fact that the whole section between lines 1000 and 1410 is a subroutine. Lines 1500 to 1630 constitute another subroutine which does the searching of the arrays. The loop is organised by a pair of FOR/NEXT lines in which the limit is set to Z, the total number of items. The code is a little more difficult to read and so the documentation is given alongside.

```
1500    FAST
1510    PRINT " SPECIFIED ITEMS "
1520    FOR J = 1 TO Z
1530    GO SUB 1800             (to select appropriate array)
1540    IF P >= L AND P <= M THEN LET E ( J ) = 1
                    (P is the value extracted from the array)
1550    IF P < L OR P > M THEN LET E ( J ) = 0
                                (rejects inappropriate elements)
```

The array E is the depository of the search. Later searches will use this array over again and so line 1550 is needed to set elements to zero if the search criteria are not met. Previous searches might have resulted in a " 1 " being stored there.

```
1560    IF E ( J ) = 1 THEN PRINT J ,
                                (signifies the item identified)
1570    NEXT J
1580    SLOW
1590    PRINT
1600    PRINT " KEY NEWLINE " (signal to clear for next search)
1610    INPUT A$
1620    CLS
1630    RETURN
```

A second search loop is needed for subsequent searches where only the elements set to 1 by the previous search are examined. This loop prints those items which meet both criteria and this list can be used to estimate correlations.

```
1700    FAST
1710    PRINT " SPECIFIED ITEMS "
1720    FOR J = 1 TO Z
1725    IF E ( J ) = 0 THEN GO TO 1750 (skip search if
                                        element empty)
```

```
1730   GO SUB 1800        (checks against new criteria)
1740   IF P >= L AND P <= M THEN PRINT J
                          (leaves previous list unchanged)
1750   NEXT J
1760   SLOW
1770   INPUT A$           (allows pause for listing data)
1780   CLS
1790   RETURN
```

And now the last working part of the program, after this menu, is all that remains to be keyed in.

```
1800   IF A < 4 THEN LET A$ = STR$ A ( J )
                          (turns number into a string)
1810   IF A > 3 AND A < 9 THEN LET A$ = STR$ B ( J )
                           see note 1
1820   IF A > 8 AND A < 12 THEN LET A$ = STR$ C ( J )
                           see note 1
1830   IF A > 11 THEN LET A$ = STR$ D ( J )   see note 1
1840   LET P = VAL A$ ( X TO Y ) (turns string back to a no.)
1850   IF A = 3 THEN LET P = P - 100  )
1860   IF A = 8 THEN LET P = P - 1    }  see note 2
1870   RETURN                         )
```

note 1: these lines select the correct array from which to extract data.

note 2: allows for the adding of " H " at lines 260, 480, 610 and 830.

This last active part of the program makes use of all the organisation that has gone on before. The variable P is set to the value of the coded information and the subroutine at line 1500 uses this to decide whether or not the item being examined fits the description. The correct array has to be chosen because the information could be stored in any of the four, A to D. At the menu where the characteristic to be studied is selected, the variable " A " is set to the choice made and this value is used here. When A is less than four, the information is held in array (A) but when A is between four and eight the machine will have to find what it's looking for in array (B).

Next, use is made of the information held in the variables X and Y. These will indicate the characters of the string containing the information being sought. The required characters are selected and the function VAL turns them into a number for use in decision making in the subroutine at line 1500.

Finally, the effect of adding 10 000 000 to each element to make sure that it contains eight characters has to be removed. The effect will only be important in those elements where digit eight holds useful information. The elements in arrays (C) and (D) have vacant eighth digits so we need only worry about (A) and (B). Lines 1850 and 1860 remove the effect of this precaution before the information is used.

All that remains now is the code for the main menu:

```
2000  PRINT TAB B ; " RECORDS "   (B is set to 10)
2010  PRINT
2020  PRINT " KEY 1 FOR INITIAL SEARCH "
2030  PRINT " KEY 2 FOR SUBSEQUENT SEARCHES "
2040  PRINT " KEY 3 TO STORE DATA "
2050  PRINT " KEY 4 TO ADD DATA "
2060  PRINT " KEY 5 TO STOP "
2070  INPUT A$
2080  CLS
2090  LET R = VAL A$
2100  IF R = 1 THEN GO SUB 1000
2110  IF R = 2 THEN PRINT " SUBSEQUENT SEARCH "
2120  IF R = 2 THEN GO SUB 1010
```

This section uses the same routine to print the same list with different headings:

```
2130  IF R = 1 THEN GO SUB 1500
2140  IF R = 2 THEN GO SUB 1700
2150  IF R = 1 OR R = 2 THEN GO TO 2000 (for the next
                                         search)
2160  IF R = 3 THEN GO TO 100
2170  IF R = 4 THEN LET J = 1
2180  IF R = 4 THEN GO TO 890
```

These last two lines allow the information on any item to be added or changed. The effect is to break into the main data input loop at the point where the next item to be described is specified.

```
2190    PRINT TAB B ; " START TAPE "
2200    PRINT AT B , B ; " KEY NEWLINE "
2210    INPUT A$
2220    CLS
2230    SAVE " RECORD "
2240    GO TO 2000
```

Which will cause the program to save itself in such a way that, when it is loaded into the machine next it will start running at the right place, without the use of RUN or GO TO commands. This protects the variables which will have been stored from accidental loss due to the use of RUN.

All through the chapter there have been references to variables which have not been set up. If the program is used before these are set, then it will crash, so they will have to be set up now. There are two choices. First there could be a set of program lines like these:

```
20      PRINT " KEY THE NUMBER OF ITEMS TO BE DESCRIBED "
21      INPUT A$
22      LET Z = VAL A$
23      DIM A ( Z )
24      DIM B ( Z )
25      DIM C ( Z )
26      DIM D ( Z )
27      DIM E ( Z )
28      LET B = 10
29      LET C = 100
30      LET D = 1000
31      LET E = 10000
32      LET F = 100000
33      LET G = 1000000
34      LET H = 10000000
```

but this would use up a lot of memory as it is stored twice, once in the program area and once in the variables store. The other alternative is to key in these lines without line numbers and then key NEWLINE to give the computer commands to obey immediately. This second method does save memory but is liable to encourage mistakes, lines could be missed out or an extra zero could be keyed. The best compromise, if you want to save the memory, is to key in the lines, check them carefully, RUN the program once and then delete the lines. The machine will have the information safely tucked up in the variables store and won't forget them. There is one problem with this method of saving the odd byte. The information will be lost if a user manages to crash the system and then uses RUN to save the situation. You will have to decide if the extra storage gained is worth this risk.

Your program is now ready for use, but what use can you make of it? In its present form only a stock controller from the mythical firm which makes these strange items could make use of it, but with a little thought, some planning and adjustment of the storage and extraction, any group of items with a large number of characteristics can be described and sorted by the machine. Pools fans might wish to make use of the program to find undreamed of links between match results and the number of anti-clockwise turnstiles at the home ground. Prison governors might want to see if the effect of educational classes for prisoners is connected in any way with re-conviction rate. It might turn out that visits from wives or the popularity rating of the prison canteen has more effect. Colleges may wish to find out which, if any, of the tests and assessments made on students, is any good as a predictor of success or failure at final examinations. A stock controller may wish to find out which items of stock will fit onto shelving with a given height, depth and load bearing capacity. One of these might fit your application or, as is more likely, none will, but the basic idea of the program is easily adapted to a multitude of applications.

VARIABLES USED IN BULK STORAGE

A and A$	Any input that need not be permanent.
D	Set to 1000, used to check that input is of the right order.
B to H	Adjusting factors from 10 to 10 000 000.
J	General loop counter.
L and M	Minimum and maximum values for a search.
P	Value extracted from storage for consideration.
R	Selection from the menu. The value of R is used by the ZX81 to guide it through the different searches.

X and Y	Point to the characters of interest in a string. X and Y are used in string slicing.
Z	The number of items in the set.

Arrays

A to D	Dimensioned to (Z), these hold all the data.
E	Dimensioned to (Z), this holds the information which is extracted from arrays A to D during searches.

9 Rank Order

It is a tedious task, adding up marks which go back several terms or even years. Many students will have missed some of the tests and so the calculation of the averages will not be straightforward. The final job of organising the students into rank order takes a surprising amount of time. This program reduces the amount of time it takes to complete these tasks and, just as important, it eliminates most of the arithmetical errors which are so embarrassing. Students, with their vested interest in the fine detail of the list and only one calculation to make, are quick to spot an error which would lift them a place or two in the list. The ZX81 is set up to cope with any number of students up to a maximum of 256. Few schools or colleges will have more than this number of students following the same course at the same time. Any number of assessments and any range of marks can be handled as long as the total marks earned stays below 10^{38}!

There are many algorithms which enable computers to bring some order to a list of numbers. The bubble sort is the example quoted in most books on programming because it is so simple. It is called "bubble" because it allows the lighter numbers in a list to bubble up to the top. It may be simple but it is slow. The Shell-Metzner sorting routine is much more efficient in every way but it is also difficult to understand. The sorting routine used in this program is simplicity itself and produces the information at least as fast as it can be written down or printed on the ZX printer. There seems little point in making it more complex.

The information is stored in single dimensional arrays. If you are interested in the ZX81's multi-dimensional array capability then you will enjoy the next program. For the moment, everything will be kept as simple as possible. Four arrays are set up in the opening lines, three to store the permanent data and one which is for the temporary storage of data before it is checked and fed into the larger arrays.

```
10      PRINT " * * * * * * * RANK ORDER PROGRAM "
                          (spaces to centralise the heading)
20      PRINT
30      PRINT " KEY THE NO. OF STUDENTS "
40      INPUT A
50      PRINT A ; " * STUDENTS "
60      DIM E ( A )       (stores total scores)
70      DIM F ( A )       (holds no. of tests taken)
80      DIM G ( A )       (for the average score)
90      DIM Y ( 10 )      (temporary pre-check storage)
100     CLS
```

It would be prudent to enter a few more than the actual number of students to allow for the arrival of newcomers. Once the arrays have been dimensioned, there is no way of increasing the space allocated without clearing the information from the smaller arrays.

Now that the storage has been arranged, it is time to limit the values to be stored in them as determined by the test and mark system that you operate.

```
110     PRINT " KEY THE NO. OF TESTS "
120     INPUT B
130     PRINT B ; " * TESTS "
140     PRINT
150     PRINT " KEY THE MAXIMUM SCORE "
160     INPUT C
170     PRINT C ; " * MARKS "
180     PRINT
```

The computer now has a means of recognising when all the information has been stored and a means of telling the difference between a missed score and a mark of zero. Any score which is greater than the maximum marks for the tests can indicate a missed test.

The main loop is the next thing to be set up. The loop will stop when the counter gets to " B ", the total number of tests to be considered.

```
190    FOR J = 1 TO B
200    PRINT " KEY SCORES FOR TEST * " ; J
210    PRINT " IN BLOCKS OF TEN "
220    PRINT
230    PRINT " IF A STUDENT HAS NO GRADE KEY * " ; C + 1
240    PRINT " KEY NEWLINE TO START "
250    INPUT A$               (the start signal)
260    CLS
```

The test scores are now loaded into a buffer array in lots of ten. The batches are checked for errors before being stored. A loop which counts up to ten is used to fill the buffer store, but before this loop is reached the student number must be organised. During the loop the ZX81 asks itself if this is the last student and it uses the student counter " L " and the loop counter " K " to decide. " L " is set to zero at first and incremented by ten each time a set of ten scores is accepted as being correct.

```
270    LET L = 0
275    PRINT " TEST * " ; J
277    PRINT
280    FOR K = 1 TO 10
285    IF L + K = A + 1 THEN GO TO 350  (last student)
290    PRINT " STUDENT * " ; L + K ,  (each student in turn)
300    INPUT S                          (the score)
305    IF S > C + 1 THEN GO TO 900      (too big)
310    LET Y(K) = S                     (loads score)
320    PRINT Y(K)                       (prints score)
330    NEXT K                           (next student)
```

Now comes the opportunity to check the typing and reject the information if there are any errors. The rejection is simple, the machine just asks for the information again and overwrites the information already stored in the temporary store.

```
340    PRINT
350    PRINT " IF THESE ARE CORRECT THEN KEY C "
360    INPUT A$
370    CLS    (the screen has to be cleared one way or
               another, why not here?)
```

So - if the signal is "mistake" the ZX81 will have to go back to 275 and wait for the information to be fed in again. If all is well then the data can be stored permanently. Line 385 allows the machine to move to a special routine if the present batch contains the last student.

```
380     IF A$ <> " C " THEN GO TO 275
385     IF L + K = A + 1 THEN GO TO 450
390     FOR K = 1 TO 10
400     IF Y(K) <> C + 1 THEN LET E ( L + K ) = E ( L + K )
+ Y ( K )
410     IF Y(K) <> C + 1 THEN LET F ( L + K ) = F ( L + K )
+ 1
420     NEXT K
```

At lines 400 and 410, as long as the score does not equal the "missed test" signal, then the score is added to the correct element in array " E ", and the number of tests that the student has completed, held in array " F ", is incremented. The loop then recycles until ten scores have been entered when:

```
430     LET L = L + 10
440     GO TO 275
```

which means, go on to the next batch of ten and call for their results.

If the batch of ten contains the last of the students, then it is unlikely that all ten students exist and less than ten marks are needed. At line 450 is a section similar to the last, which deals with the last few students neatly.

```
450     FOR M = 1 TO A - L
460     IF Y(M) <> C + 1 THEN LET E(L + M) = E(L + M) + Y(M)
470     IF Y(M) <> C + 1 THEN LET F(L + M ) = F(L + M ) + 1
480     NEXT M
```

Which polishes off the last few neatly and clears the way for the next section which is a menu.

```
500     CLS
510     PRINT " ALL SCORES NOW IN FOR TEST * " ; J
520     PRINT
```

```
530    PRINT " KEY C TO STORE THE NEXT TEST SCORES "
540    PRINT " KEY S TO STOP AND FILE DATA "
550    INPUT A$
560    IF A$ = " C " THEN GO TO 590  (you have probably
                                       forgotten about J)
570    IF A$ = " S " THEN GO TO 1000
580    GO TO 500
590    NEXT J
```

At line 560 we finally come to the end of the loop which started at line 190. The opportunity to store the information collected to date is given here. This means that the data can be fed into the program at several points in the course. The machine will remember where it had got to each time and start up at the correct place next time the program·is loaded. Now to sort out the data. The first job is to find all the average marks and the machine will do this very quickly in fast mode.

```
600    FAST
610    FOR N = 1 TO A
620    LET G(N) = E(N) * ( 100/C ) / ( F(N) + .001 )
630    NEXT N
640    SLOW
650    CLS
```

The 0.001 in line 620 is to avoid overloading the ZX81's arithmetic. If a student leaves the college before taking any tests, then he will cause the machine to divide by zero. If this happens the computer will stop and show an arithmetic overflow report. After all this frantic arithmetic we can relax in slow mode and watch the information print smoothly on the screen as the computer works its way through this final segment of the program. This is the simple sorting routine that you were promised earlier on. The machine counts to a hundred, pausing at each number to look for any students with an average mark of the same value. All such students are printed in a list. The 0.5 in line 740 is added to the array element before the integer value is taken, so that the nearest whole number will be considered.

```
700    LET P = 0
710    PRINT " THESE STUDENTS SCORED AN AVERAGE OF * " ;
P ; " * MARKS "
720    PRINT
730    FOR N = 1 TO A
```

```
740    IF INT ( G(N) + .5 ) = P THEN PRINT " STUDENT * " ;
N , " * ON * " ; F(N) ; " * TESTS "
750    NEXT N
760    INPUT A$
```

And that's all there is to the sort. The last line allows the user to jot down the information before pressing NEWLINE to go onto the next average score. You might wish to modify this section for the ZX printer and replace the print statements with LPRINT commands. Once the signal is given then the ZX81 adds one to the counter, clears the screen and then checks to see if it has reached the end of the series. It then either goes on to another test or gives you the opportunity to file the data.

```
770    LET P = P + 1
780    CLS
790    IF P = 101 THEN GO TO 540
800    GO TO 710
```

You will probably have forgotten that the computer was sent to line 900 if a score was too large at line 305. Now is the time to do something about the mistake:

```
900    PRINT " SCORE TOO HIGH "
910    PRINT " TRY AGAIN * " ; L + K ,
920    GO TO 300
```

And finally, the auto start routine:

```
1000   CLS
1010   LET X = 1            (see below)
1020   PRINT AT 10 , 10 ; " START TAPE "
1030   PRINT TAB 10 ; " KEY NEWLINE "
1035   INPUT A$
1040   CLS
1050   SAVE " RANK "
1060   IF X <> 1 THEN RUN
1070   GO TO 500
```

Before you save the final copy for use, key: LET X = 0, NEWLINE. Prepare the tape for recording and then key: GO TO 1020, NEWLINE. When the program is saved, the value held by X will not be one and so the program will RUN and set itself up on the first loading. Next time the program is used X will be set to one at line 1010 and so the computer will go to line 500 for its instructions. This way the variables will be safe but an initial RUN will be achieved.

This is a straightforward program with no frills. If a student missed a test and then caught up later, there is no provision for the storage of this late information. The adjustment will have to be made by hand when the results are printed. Rank Order is, however, easy to key in, quick to load and simple to use. The program which follows is equally simple to use but allows for more contingencies. As payment for this extra sophistication, the later program is longer and more complex.

VARIABLES USED IN RANK ORDER

A	Number of students.
B	Number of tests.
C	Maximum possible marks in any test.
J to N	Various counters for loops.
S	Holds each score before storage.
P	Used to display the score in the final Rank Order list.

Arrays

E(A)	Array to hold students' total scores.
F(A)	Array to hold number of tests students have sat.
G(A)	Array to hold students' average scores.
Y(10)	Temporary storage buffer.

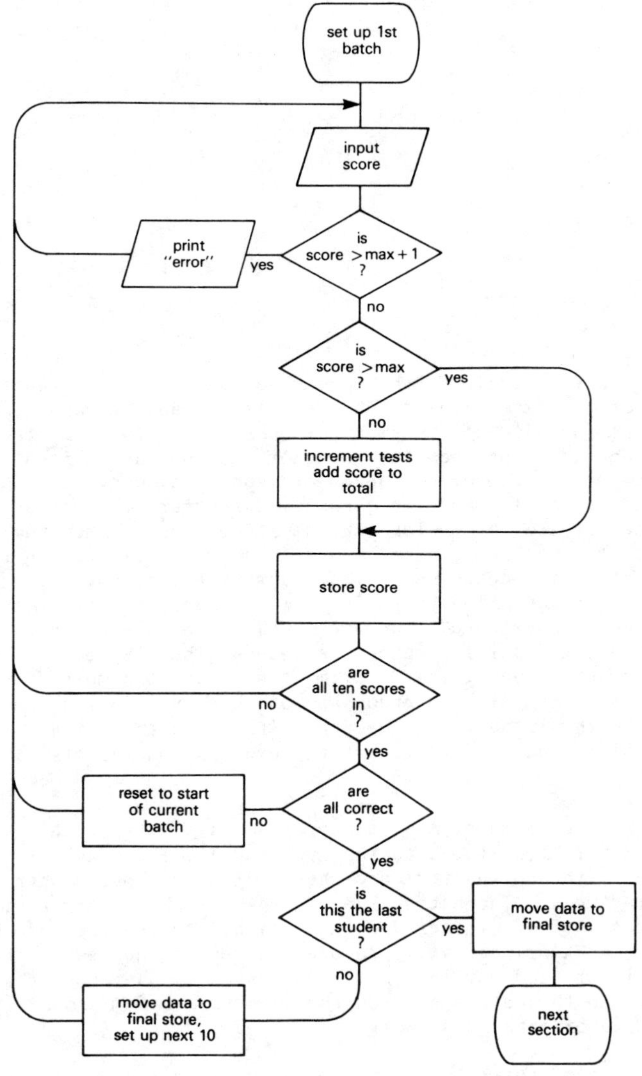

Figure 9.1 Rank order flow chart

10 Exam Result Analysis

Right in the middle of the summer holiday, everyone wants to know about the exam results. The headmaster wants to know the overall performance of the examination students in terms that will answer the questions from the governors and on the basis of which he can report to the press. Heads of department want to know about the students' performance in the subjects offered by the department. The curriculum development committee need to know how the last bit of fine tuning of the curriculum was reflected in the balance of exam success and failure across the school. Even the Department of Education and Science want some information and, as might have been expected, the work that has been done for all the other interested parties cannot be reused. The DES need a subtly different set of data. The Department need a 10% sample of your results and make this as random as possible by choosing the students with birthdays on the 5th, 15th and 25th of the month. The school is required to report the examination results of these students.

The Exam Performance Analysis program will extract this information and more from the data that you key in. The exam entries are keyed in in the Spring term and the results are loaded when they arrive in August. The extraction job which took so long previously is now the work of minutes and the reliability is likely to be improved. A ZX printer will produce the reports needed by the various interested parties in a form that will photocopy for circulation and the data stored on the tape is a safeguard against the loss of the original paperwork.

The program stores the information in two dimensional string arrays. The data is extracted by means of the ZX81's string slicing ability and the CODEs of the characters stored in the arrays are used to compare one result with another. The system is designed to deal with an exam group of 256 students and there is enough space to allow up to 16 exam entries. The co-educational comprehensive school has been used as a model and so the machine asks how many boys there are and then how many girls. The results are stored separately in order that teachers can keep an eye on the effects of their attempts to improve the girls' maths and science results and the boys' language and humanities performance.

The user is given the opportunity to set up only the space needed for the particular exam set and therefore keep the load and save time to a minimum. The loading of the entries will take place in term time and so an opportunity has been given to store the data onto tape at any stage during the run. The keying in of the results will take place during the holiday and interruptions are less likely so the machine asks for the information all in one go. This saves some time and some space but there is no reason why an escape routine should not be added to this stage and the earlier one can act as a model.

In the previous program, Rank Order, the data was stored in a buffer array for checking before it was accepted for inclusion. Here, an alternative method is explored. The data is fed straight into its final destination. If a mistake is discovered then the relevant section of the information is deleted and replaced with space characters by a short section of code. Another alternative which is offered here for your consideration is concerned with keying in a date. In the financial programs, the date was fed in as a set of three numbers. Here the date is requested as a six digit number. The ZX81 reads it as a string, slices it up into three pairs of characters, and then presents it as a date is conventionally written. If you find this method suits you better than the alternative, then it can be extended for programs which use the date in arithmetic by taking the VAL of each two character slice. For the purposes of the Department's statistics, only two digits are needed but the full date of birth has been stored as it might be thought useful to compare the exam performance of the younger students with the results of their older classmates.

The first section of the program deals with the setting up of the system and requires little comment except that at line 200 there is a subroutine which checks for typing errors.

```
10      PRINT " SETTING UP THE SYSTEM "
20      PRINT
30      PRINT
40      PRINT " KEY MAXIMUM NUMBER OF EXAM ENTRIES PER
STUDENT " ,
50      INPUT X
```

```
60      PRINT X
70      PRINT " KEY NUMBER OF GIRLS * ";
80      INPUT G
90      PRINT G
100     PRINT " KEY NUMBER OF BOYS *  ";
110     INPUT B
120     PRINT B
130     DIM G$ ( G , 2 * X + 6 )
140     DIM B$ ( B , 2 * X + 6 )
150     GO SUB 200
160     IF A$ <> " C " THEN GO TO 10  (C means all OK)
170     GO TO 2000     (section which starts loading data)
```

The girls' and boys' storage strings are dimensioned to the number of students in one direction and to the number of characters needed to hold the data on any student in the other. One character is needed for the exam code and another for the result. A further six characters are needed to hold the date of birth. This will explain the "G, 2 * X ± 6" bit in line 130.

In the example, the maximum number of exam entries is eleven. Only one of the three students shown has taken the maximum. In two dimensional strings, the first figure in the dimension statement determines the number of strings to be set up and the second number sets them all to the same, specified length. If they are only partly filled then the rest of the space is filled with space characters. CSE results are quoted in figures while O level boards use letters. The machine differentiates between the two exams on this basis as well.

Here is how the data is organised inside the computer:

	Student 1	Student 2	Student 3
Day	0	3	2
	4	0	1
Month	0	1	0
	9	1	6
Year	6	6	6
	5	5	6
Exam 1	A	A	A
Result	C	4	D
Exam 2	B	B	B
Result	C	3	E
Exam 3	C	D	E
Result	A	6	C
	⋮	⋮	⋮
Exam 10	H	J	H
Result	2	2	3
Exam 11	–	K	–
Result	–	A	–

The next section of the listing contains most of the sub-routines. The first one is the familiar "typing error" routine:

```
200    PRINT
201    PRINT " KEY C IF THESE ARE OK OTHERWISE NEWLINE "
202    INPUT A$
203    CLS
204    RETURN
```

And next, a long routine which loads the information into the arrays. This routine is called by some code at line 2000. This code does an organising job, calling many subroutines which do the donkey work.

```
220    PRINT
230    PRINT " KEY : EXAM CODE  [N/L]  LEVEL  [N/L] "
                               (N/L In inverse)
240    PRINT " KEY Z AFTER LAST EXAM "
250    PRINT " KEY S TO RECORD DATA SO FAR "
255    PRINT
260    PRINT " EXAM " , " LEVEL "
```

All of which simply prints up a set of keying in instructions and some headings for the data when it is printed. The loop which fills each of the arrays in B$ and G$ uses " K " as its counter. The exam information fits into the array after the date of birth so the counter starts at 7 to load the array from character 7 onwards. The length of the array is determined by the maximum number of exams entered, " X " and so the first line in the loop is:

```
270    FOR K = 7 TO 2 * X + 6 STEP 2
280    INPUT A$                    (the code of the exam)
290    IF CODE A$ < 38 OR CODE A$ > 63 THEN PRINT " ERROR " ;
300    IF CODE A$ < 38 OR CODE A$ > 63 THEN GO TO 280
```

These last two lines reject all input that is not in the form of letters. " A " has a code of 38 and " Z " has a code of 63.

```
310    IF A$ = " Z " THEN LET K = 2 * X + 6
320    IF A$ = " Z " THEN GO TO 460
325    IF A$ = " S " THEN GO TO 6000
```

310 and 320 allow you to go on to the next student if this one has less exam entries than the maximum. The computer automatically goes to the next student if the maximum is keyed in. Line 325 allows you to file the data entered so far.

```
330    IF J > G THEN GO TO 360
```

No, there isn't a mistake, J is right. J is the counter set up at line 2000 which counts through the students and if it has counted through more than the number of girls, then the next information must be about one of the boys. The boys' information is stored by line 360 and the next line looks after girls' data.

```
340    LET G$ ( J , K ) = CHR$  CODE A$
350    GO TO 370              (to by-pass the boys' bit)
```

Line 340 is not exactly straightforward. "G$ (J , K) " means the element in the girls' array, which stores data on student J and which is K characters from the start. CHR$ CODE A$ seems a long-winded way of getting the information in, but it ensures that only one character is loaded. The CODE of A$ is the code of the first character and so loading CHR$ CODE A$ does not over fill the array if someone insists on keying "English" when all that is needed is " E ".

```
360    LET B$ ( J - G , K ) = CHR$  CODE A$
```

If the number of girls is deducted from the student number of this boy, then the result is his element number in the boys' array.

```
370    PRINT CHR$ CODE A$ ,
380    INPUT A$         (" C " for CSE or " O " for O level)
390    IF A$ <> " O " AND A$ <> " C " THEN PRINT " ERROR * ";
400    IF A$ <> " O " AND A$ <> " C " THEN GO TO 380
410    PRINT A$
420    IF J > G THEN GO TO 450
430    LET G$ ( J , K + 1 ) = A$
440    GO TO 460        (to by-pass the boys again)
```

" K + 1 " this time because the characrer has to go into the array, one further on than the exam code character.

```
450    LET B$ ( J - G , K + 1 ) = A$
```

```
460     NEXT K
470     RETURN
```

This final subroutine clears an array of errors and replaces them with space characters:

```
510     FOR K = 1 TO 2 * X + 6
520     IF J > G THEN GO TO 550
530     LET G$ ( J , K ) = " * "
540     GO TO 560
550     LET B$ ( J - G , K ) = " * "
560     NEXT K
570     RETURN
```

The main menu will need no explanation:

```
1000    PRINT TAB 7 ; " THREADNEEDLE STREET SCHOOL "
1010    PRINT " * * EXAM PERFORMANCE ANALYSIS "
1020    PRINT
1030    PRINT " KEY 1 TO SET UP SYSTEM "
1040    PRINT " KEY 2 TO STORE RESULTS "
1050    PRINT " KEY 3 TO STOP "
1060    PRINT " KEY 4 FOR DOB SORT "
1070    PRINT " KEY 5 FOR SUBJECT SORT "
1080    PRINT " KEY 6 FOR RESULTS SORT "
1100    INPUT A$
1110    CLS
1120    IF A$ = " 1 " THEN GO TO 10
1130    IF A$ = " 2 " THEN GO TO 2400
1140    IF A$ = " 3 " THEN GO TO 5000
1150    IF A$ = " 4 " THEN GO TO 3000
1160    IF A$ = " 5 " THEN GO TO 3500
1170    IF A$ = " 6 " THEN GO TO 4000
1180    GO TO 1000
```

This next segment of the program does a foreman's job, organising the work of the subroutines:

```
2000   CLS
2010   FOR J = 1 TO G
2020   PRINT " * * * ENTERING GIRLS EXAMS "
2025   PRINT " STUDENT NO * " ; J
2030   GO SUB 220                               (load entries)
2040   GO SUB 200                               (check typing)
2050   IF A$ <> " C " THEN GO SUB 500           (clear errors)
2055   IF A$ <> " C " THEN LET J = J - 1        (back 1 to reload)
2060   IF A$ <> " C " THEN GO TO 2160
2065   GO SUB 2200                              (date of birth)
2070   NEXT J
```

And now a "forelady" to look after the boys:

```
2100   FOR J = G + 1 TO G + B
2110   PRINT " ENTERING BOYS EXAMS "
2115   PRINT " STUDENT NO * " ; J
2120   GO SUB 220
2130   GO SUB 200
2140   IF A$ <> " C " THEN GO SUB 500
2145   IF A$ <> " C " THEN LET J = J - 1
2150   IF A$ <> " C " THEN GO TO 2160
2155   GO SUB 2200
2160   NEXT J
2170   GO TO 1000                               (the main menu)
```

To finish off the preliminary part of the program, here is the final subroutine which loads the date of birth of each student:

```
2200   PRINT " KEY DATE OF BIRTH AS A SIX FIGURE NUMBER.
EG. FOR THE FIRST OF APR 1965 KEY 010465 "
2210   INPUT D$
2215   IF LEN D$ <> 6 THEN GO TO 2210           (checks for 6
                                                 characters)
2220   CLS
```

```
2230   PRINT D$ ( 1 TO 2 ) ; " / " ; D$ ( 3 TO 4 ) ; " / " ;
D$ ( 5 TO )
2240   GO SUB 200                    (typing mistake?)
2250   IF A$ <> " C " THEN GO TO 2200
2260   IF J > G THEN GO TO 2290
2270   LET G$ ( J , TO 6 ) = D$
2280   GO TO 2300
2290   LET B$ ( J - G , TO 6 ) = D$
2300   RETURN
```

We are now about half way through and almost at the end of the part which stores the data. The lines which follow cover the loading of the exam results into the ZX81. The FOR/NEXT loops which count through each student's array in steps of two are given limits of " 2 * X + 5 " to avoid overloading the arrays. The other point which needs some discussion is that string slicing has to be used to isolate a character in one of the arrays. At first I tried:

```
IF G$ ( J , K ) = " A " THEN ......
```

but soon found that it is necessary to use:

```
IF G$ ( J , K TO K ) = " A " THEN ......
```

In all other respects this section is quite transparent:

```
2400   CLS
2410   FOR J = 1 TO G
2420   PRINT " ENTERING GIRLS RESULTS "
2430   PRINT
2440   PRINT " STUDENT * " ; J
2450   PRINT
2460   FOR K = 7 TO 2 * X + 5 STEP 2
2470   IF G$ ( J , K TO K ) = " * " THEN LET K = 2 * X + 6
2480   IF G$ ( J , K TO K ) = " * " THEN GO TO 2540
```

These last two lines set the counter to the end of the loop and call NEXT K when the last entry has been read and the rest of the array is full of spaces.

```
2490   PRINT G$ ( J , K TO K ) ,          (prints exam code)
2500   INPUT A$
2510   IF LEN A$ <> 1 THEN GO TO 2500   (only 1 character)
2520   PRINT A$
2530   LET G$ ( J , K + 1 ) = A$          (stores result)
2540   NEXT K
2550   GO SUB 200                         (typing errors?)
2560   IF A$ <> " C " THEN GO TO 2420    (C means OK)
2565   NEXT J
```

As before, the boys are dealt with after the girls by means of a similar section of code:

```
2570   FOR J = 1 TO B
2580   PRINT " ENTERING BOYS RESULTS "
2590   PRINT
2600   PRINT " STUDENT * " ; J + G
2610   PRINT
2620   FOR K = 7 TO 2 * X + 5 STEP 2
2630   IF B$ ( J , K TO K ) = " * " THEN LET K = 2 * X + 6
2640   IF B$ ( J , K TO K ) = " * " THEN GO TO 2700
```

As you will remember, this moves the computer on to the next student if the present student has had all his results stored.

```
2650   PRINT B$ ( J , K TO K ) ,
2660   INPUT A$
2670   IF LEN A$ <> 1 THEN GO TO 2660   (only 1 character)
2680   PRINT A$
2690   LET B$ ( J , K + 1 ) = A$          (loads result)
2700   NEXT K
2710   GO SUB 200                         (typing errors?)
2720   IF A$ <> " C " THEN GO TO 2580
2725   NEXT J
2730   GO TO 1000    (back to the menu after all that exam
                      result storage)
```

The raw material is now assembled and it can be sorted and re-arranged according to your needs. We might as well get the legal requirements out of the way first, so lets go straight into the "Date of Birth" sort.

```
3000   CLS        (it's good housekeeping to keep the screen
                   clear after each section)
3010   PRINT TAB 10 ; " DOB SORT "
3020   PRINT
3030   FOR J = 1 TO G + B  (sorting through the whole lot)
3040   IF J > G THEN GO TO 3100  (go onto the boys section)
3050   IF G$ ( J , 2 TO 2 ) <> " 5 " THEN GO TO 3170
```

All students with a five in the second digit of their date of birth must have been born on either the 5th, 15th or the 25th of the month, so if the second digit is not a five, then the student is of no interest to the DES. The command at line 3170 is NEXT J, calling for the next student.

```
3060   PRINT " STUDENT * " ; J ; " * RESULTS "
3070   FOR K = 7 TO 2 * X + 6
3080   PRINT G$ ( J , K TO K ) ,
3090   GO TO 3130                    (just NEXT K)
```

The loop prints out the contents of the student's array after her date of birth, organised into a column of exam codes and a column of corresponding results.

```
3100   IF B$ ( J - G , 2 TO 2 ) <> " 5 " THEN GO TO 3170
3105   PRINT " STUDENT * " ; J ; " * RESULTS "
3110   FOR K = 7 TO 2 * X + 6
3120   PRINT B$ ( J - G , K TO K ) ,
3130   NEXT K
```

This is just a very similar segment which prints out the boys' results.

```
3135   PRINT
3140   PRINT " KEY NEWLINE FOR NEXT STUDENT "
3150   INPUT A$                      (the signal to carry on)
3160   CLS
```

```
3170   NEXT J                        (the next student)
3180   GO TO 1000                    (the main menu)
```

The next part of the system allows the user to count the number of students who gained a particular grade on a particular exam, or who gained grades within a particular range of grades. The exam and the range of results that the ZX81 will be searching for can be specified at the keyboard. After the search, the machine returns to the main menu but the entry of a "5" will allow another search.

```
3500   CLS
3510   PRINT " * * * PERFORMANCE AT EACH EXAM "
3520   PRINT
3530   PRINT " KEY EXAM CODE "
3540   INPUT C$
3545   PRINT C$
3550   PRINT " KEY MAXIMUM GRADE * " ;
3560   INPUT M$
3565   PRINT M$
3570   PRINT " KEY MINIMUM GRADE * ";
3580   INPUT L$
3585   PRINT L$
3590   GO SUB 200                    (typing errors?)
3595   IF A$ <> " C " THEN GO TO 3500
3600   CLS
```

Now comes the first bit of fast action in this program. The ZX81 will search through its arrays until it finds a student with an exam result in the correct subject and within the specified range. When the student is found, one is added to the counter " N " before the machine goes onto the next student.

```
3605   FAST
3610   LET N = 0
3620   FOR J = 1 TO G + B
3630   FOR K = 7 TO 5 + 2 * X STEP 2
3640   IF J > G THEN GO TO 3680  (to by-pass the girls)
3650   IF G$ ( J , K TO K ) <> C$ THEN GO TO 3710
```

which means, if the exam code stored in this array element is not the code of the one being looked for, go onto the next exam.

```
3660    LET A = CODE G$ ( J , K + 1 TO K + 1 )
```

Which turns the character into a value for comparison.

```
3670    GO TO 3700                  (to by-pass the boys)
3680    IF B$ ( J - G , K TO K ) <> C$ THEN GO TO 3710
3690    LET A = CODE B$ ( J - G , K + 1 TO K + 1 )
3700    IF A <= CODE L$ AND A >= CODE M$ THEN LET N = N + 1
```

Or...If the exam code doesn't match the specification, by-pass this one. Otherwise, extract the result of the exam and, if it is within the allowed range, add one to the counter. " <= " and " >= " *are* the right way round.

```
3710    NEXT K
3720    NEXT J
3730    SLOW
```

These lines finish off the search and return the computer to slow mode to allow smooth display of its handiwork.

```
3740    PRINT N ; " * STUDENTS GAINED GRADES BETWEEN " ; L$ ;
" * AND * " ; M$
3750    PRINT
3760    PRINT " KEY NEWLINE TO CONTINUE "
3770    INPUT A$            (signals readiness to carry on)
3780    CLS
3790    GO TO 1000          (back to the menu)
```

The results of the sorting so far have been a little impersonal. The next data search names names, or at least names the students' reference numbers. This is offered as an alternative to the earlier reporting method, giving only the number of students within the category. If a list of students is needed then the "Performance at Each Exam" routine can be easily modified in line with the pattern of this next sort.

Headmasters need to know the number of "O" level passes at each grade for the various reports on exam success that have to be made. Included amongst the "O" level ABC pass grades are all the grade 1

CSE passes which are equivalent to passes at "O" level.

```
4000   CLS
4010   PRINT " * * * * * O LEVEL ABC/1 SORT "
4020   PRINT
4030   PRINT " KEY THE NUMBER OF PASSES * " ;
4035   INPUT N
4040   PRINT N
4045   PRINT
4050   PRINT " THESE GIRLS GAINED * " , N ; " * PASSES AT
O LEVEL "
4055   FAST
```

And now that the limits of the search are set and the ZX81 is in fast mode, the searching can go ahead quickly. The computer looks through each student's exam results, checking to see if they are within the limits. Each time one is found, the machine adds one to the counter "A". After checking each student, the ZX81 tries matching the number of passes specified at line 4035. If it is successful it prints the student's number in the list. In any case the machine resets "A" to zero for the next student. That's what is required. Here is how the ZX81 does it:

```
4060   FOR J = 1 TO G + B  (to check all the students in one
                            go)
4070   LET A = 0
4080   FOR K = 7 TO 2 * X + 5 STEP 2
4090   IF J > G THEN GO TO 4120  (to by-pass the girls)
4100   LET A$ = G$ ( J , K + 1 TO K + 1 )
4110   GO TO 4130                (to by-pass the boys)
4120   LET A$ = B$( J-G, K+1 TO K+1)
4130   IF A$ = " A " OR A$ = " B " OR A$ = " C " OR A$
" 1 " THEN LET A = A + 1
4140   NEXT K
4150   IF A = N THEN PRINT J ,
4160   IF J = G THEN GO TO 4300
```

and at 4300 the computer will find instructions to print a new heading to separate the girls from the boys.

```
4170   NEXT J
4175   SLOW
4180   PRINT " KEY NEWLINE TO CONTINUE "
4190   INPUT A$              (the signal to carry on)
4200   CLS
4210   GO TO 1000            (THE MAIN MENU)
```

And to finish off this section:

```
4300   PRINT
4310   PRINT " THESE BOYS GAINED * " ; N , " PASSES AT
0 LEVEL "
4330   GO TO 4170
```

All that remains is to organise the automatic start up of the program and in this case, there are two auto restart routines. One is a general routine which sends the control of the program to the menu at line 1000. The second allows the user to return to the feeding in of the exam entries after a break.

```
5000   CLS
5010   PRINT AT 10, 10;" START TAPE "
5020   PRINT TAB 10; " KEY NEWLINE "
5030   INPUT A$
5040   CLS
5050   SAVE " EXAM "
5060   GO TO 1000
```

And now the alternative "auto start" routine:

```
6000   CLS
6010   PRINT AT 10 , 10 ; " START TAPE "
6020   PRINT TAB 10 ; " KEY NEWLINE "
6030   INPUT A$
6040   CLS
6050   SAVE " EXAM "
6060   PRINT " STUDENT * " ; J
6070   GO TO 220
```

This sets up the screen with the headings and promts, and allows the user to carry on keying in the exam entries as if the run was never interrupted.

That completes the listing but, before going onto the next program, it is necessary to think a little about the organisation of the data before the loading is started. All the exams that your students enter must be coded from A to Y. Z cannot be used as it is the signal for the end of a student's data. This allows for fifty different exams, twenty-five each at CSE and "O" level. Exams at these different levels, which are closely related, CSE maths and "O" level maths for example, can obviously share a code. To make best use of the codes available, there is no reason why "O" level German and CSE rural science should not use the same code, if there is no student taking CSE German or "O" level rural science.

The other task that must be done before using the program is to allocate numbers to all the students taking exams. It may be wise to add a few imaginary students to both the girls' list and the boys', to allow for late arrivals at the school who wish to take some exams with the rest. When these students come up, they can be dealt with by keying "Z" immediately, and by giving them the first of January as birthdays, to keep them out of the DOB sort. If some late comers arrive, then adopt the following procedure to include them in the system:

1) Key "3" at the menu and start the SAVE routine but press BREAK right away to interrupt the machine and make the listing available.
2) Key LET J = and then the new student's number.
3) Key GO TO 2020 for a girl or GO TO 2110 for a boy.
4) Enter the data and when asked for the next student's details;
5) Press SHIFT and RUBOUT to remove one of the quotes.
6) Press SHIFT and STOP to obtain the listing again.
7) Prepare a tape, start recording, and then key GO TO 5000 and then save the program in the normal way.

One final word about the "subject sort" at line 3500. It is not possible to search for both "O" level grades and CSE grades at the same time. The codes of the characters are used to decide if the grades are within the limits, and high exam grades have low codes. This is the reason for the symbols in line 3700 seeming to be the wrong way round. The code of the character of any grade at CSE will be lower than the code of any at "O" level. All CSE grades will therefore seem to the machine to be higher than "O" level grades. If you analyse "O" levels and CSEs separately, then no difficulty arises. The only case where the two could be connected is the equivalence of a CSE grade 1 pass and an "O" level, and this is dealt with in the O level ABC/1 sort routine.

VARIABLES USED IN THE EXAM RESULT ANALYSIS

A$	Temporary signalling.
D$	Date in six characters.
C$	Exam code.
L$	Minimum grade.
M$	Maximum grade.

G$	Main storage area. G$ is set up in two dimensions, one dimension is set to the number of girls and the second is set to twice the number of exams plus six.
B$	A similar string which looks after the boys.
B	The number of boys.
G	The number of girls.
J	Loop counter to count through the students.
K	Loop counter to count through the exams.
N	Number of passes at "O" level.
X	Maximum number of entries per student.
Z	"Last exam for this student" signal.

11 Hardware Modifications

These are all very simple modifications. They require no more electronic expertise than the ability to solder neatly. None of the programs in the other chapters require any of these modifications in order to make them run smoothly, but each suggestion more than pays for the small amount of trouble involved.

POWER SUPPLY

The Sinclair power supply gives an output of 9 volts DC via a 3.5 mm jack plug, with the tip of the plug positive. It is very convenient because all the works are contained within its very large, plug type body. The only lead is the 9 volt supply to the ZX81. If you bought a ZX81 kit without a power supply and wish to build one, then this one has definite advantages. If you have a power supply and plan to use your computer for long periods, you might still consider the four or five pounds that the components will cost, worth spending for the following reason.

The ZX81 voltage regulator is provided with a small heat sink which gets very hot. It is reasonable to assume that a machine which works at a high temperature and does a particular job, will not be as reliable as one which does the same job at a much lower temperature. The ZX81 will work as long as it is fed with DC current at a voltage between seven and eleven volts. The higher the feed voltage, the harder the voltage regulator has to work to drop it down to the five volts needed by the chips. The more work it has to do the hotter it gets and, as likely as not, the shorter will be the mean time between failures of the ZX81, baking quietly in all this waste heat. If the power pack were designed to deliver the minimum of seven volts, then all would be well until the first power crisis, when the mains voltage is dropped by twenty or so volts. This would drop the output of the power pack below the seven volts required and switch off the machine. A good compromise is to design a power pack to run at eight volts. This has a significant cooling effect.

Some users have reported a mains pack failure after running the computer for long periods of time. The fuse inside the power pack fails and is difficult to replace because it is soldered in place. Another problem which has been mentioned is that the power supply issued with the machine sometimes causes a slow ripple to pass through the picture. The more meaty, lower voltage power supply eliminates the ripple effect from those machines which suffer from it, and at the same time is less likely to blow fuses.

You will need:

1) **line supply-to-8V transformer rated at 2A**

1) rectifier bridge circuit rated at 2 amps, 50 p.i.v.

1) 2000 μF electrolytic capacitor with a working voltage of at least 16 volts

1) 1 amp fuse and fuse holder.

If you are not too sure about building electrical equipment, then you should get an electrician to check over the power pack before you plug it in. You will be dealing with mains voltage and this can be very dangerous. The main things to check are that the transformer is connected the right way round, and that the tip of the plug to the ZX81 is positive. If the thick wires of the transformer are connected across the mains, then the ZX81 will blow up before the fuse has a chance to blow! Make sure that the thin wires of the primary coil are connected to the mains. Most transformers will have the primary and secondary connections marked.

The two amp rating on all the components takes into account the possibility of further peripherals being developed for the ZX81. These are appearing on the market at the time of writing and, by the time you read this, reviews should have appeared in the computing magazines. Many of these devices offer possibilities for the users who are interested in making the ZX81 work for its living and so it is wise to make provision for the power demands they will make. To comply with the relevant safety regulations, the unit must be mounted in a stout plastic (*not* metal) box, and all mains-carrying terminals must be insulated as well. The unit should be connected to the mains via a fused plug, fitted with a 1 amp or a 3 amp fuse.

When you have finished the power pack and wish to check the voltage and polarity of the plug, don't be alarmed at the high voltage reading on your multi-meter. The voltage will drop to its normal level when the power pack is loaded.

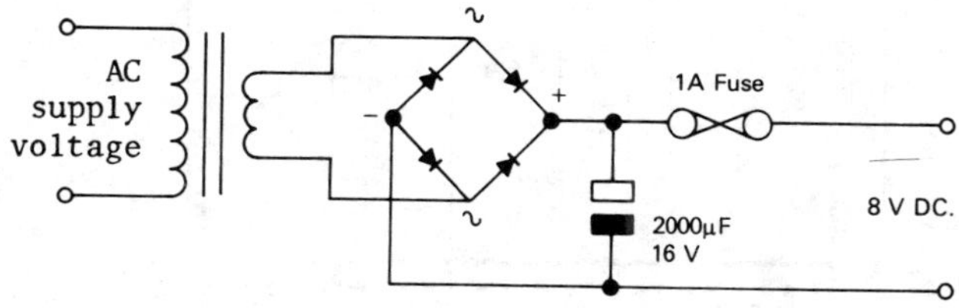
AC
supply
voltage
1A Fuse
2000μF
16 V
8 V DC.

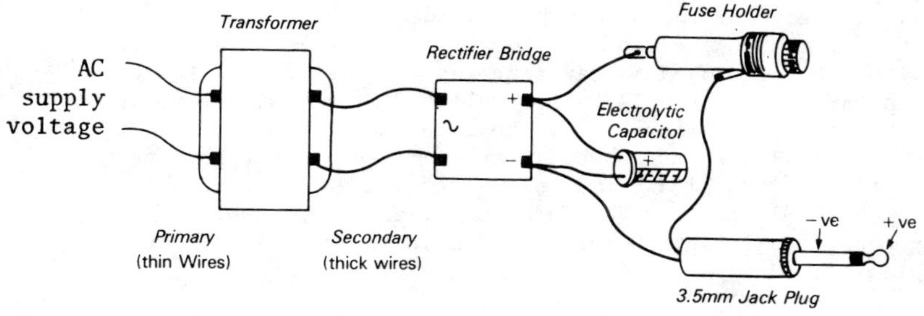
Transformer
AC
supply
voltage
Primary
(thin Wires)
Secondary
(thick wires)
Rectifier Bridge
Fuse Holder
Electrolytic
Capacitor
– ve
+ ve
3.5mm Jack Plug

EXTRA MEMORY

At first, when the ZX81 was introduced, it was thought that the 3K RAM pack that many ZX80 users possessed would not work on the ZX81. A very minor modification to the printed circuit will make the extension work on both the ZX80 and ZX81. Remove the three plastic rivets and take off the back half of the case. The chips will now be visible and it is important to work on the side of the board where you can see the components.

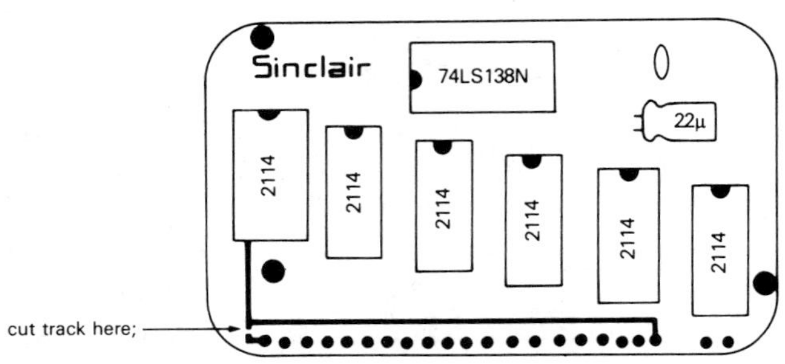

All that is needed to make the 3K RAM pack work on *both* machines is to cut the track shown. To test the modification, plug in the pack, switch on and key in the following line:

```
10    DIM A ( 102 , 6 )
```

and RUN the program. You should be rewarded with a report code 0/10 indicating that the array of 612 numbers (102 × 6) has been successfully set up. Such an array requires at least 3060 bytes of space in the RAM. On the ZX80 the smaller RAM pack will give 4K of memory but the ZX81 switches off the 1K of memory on the main board when the extra RAM is attached. If the RAM pack is plugged in permanently the two 2114 chips can be removed and used in a 3K memory board. (Just a thought for those readers who have a small memory pack with less than the full complement of six 2114 chips installed!)

If you thought that the previous modification was simple, what will you think of the next? The press has been full of reports of programs being lost from the ZX81 whilst the 16K RAM pack is in place. The main cause of this problem seems to be the fact that the RAM pack is mounted at 90^0 to the main board and is thus liable to move a little on its mounting points. The lead in the solder coating of the edge connector contacts will become coated with lead oxide quite quickly and make the surface conduct badly in places. Slight movement of the RAM pack on a less than scrupulously clean solder track causes momentary loss of power and more than momentary loss of program. There are three cures. The first is to fit the ZX81 with "radio spares" self-adhesive feet. These lift the computer high enough to ensure that the RAM pack is clear of the ground and the connector is not flexed when you press the keys. This is usually a complete cure for RAM problems. The second is to steady the RAM pack on its mountings with a piece of plasticine between the back of the computer and the front of the RAM pack. The appearance of the second cure is a little less technical than might be desired but the improvement in reliability is worth all the odd comments from onlookers. The third cure will be given in detail under the heading "eliminating the tangle".

A PROPER KEYBOARD

The low cost of the ZX81 is, to a considerable extent, due to the low cost of the keyboard. There are advantages to the installation of a normal keyboard; there is more room for "person sized" fingers and it is possible to "touch type" on a keyboard which is not almost completely flat. There are on offer, several bleepers which indicate to the typist each time a keystroke has been successful. Such annoying devices would be unnecessary if you could feel a key making contact.

Keyboards specially designed for the ZX81 are sold by several manufacturers, and these are in general the best bet. From time to time you will come across old keyboards in junk shops, on jumble sale stands at computer shows, or in surplus stores. Most of these are coded in some way and need to be stripped down to remove the intricate interconnections of the keys under the board. If you attempt such a job, make sure that no hidden connections remain, by checking *all* the keys with a multimeter for each keystroke.

When the keyboard has been stripped down so that it is no more than a set of isolated switches, it can be wired up as shown in the diagram (Figure 11.4). Choose two contacts per key from the several you will probably have and use the same two on every key. Connect up one set of contacts as shown in the top diagram and connect the second set up as shown in the lower drawing. If you wish, you can make extra keys available if there are more than forty buttons on your board. These could form a number pad with an extra decimal point if you intend doing a lot of number work on the computer. Bring out the fly leads and connect them to the underside of the computer board as shown. The connections will be easier to sort out if you can use a different colour for each connection. If you use the underside of the board, then the original keyboard will still function and the two can be used together if required. This might be useful for games.

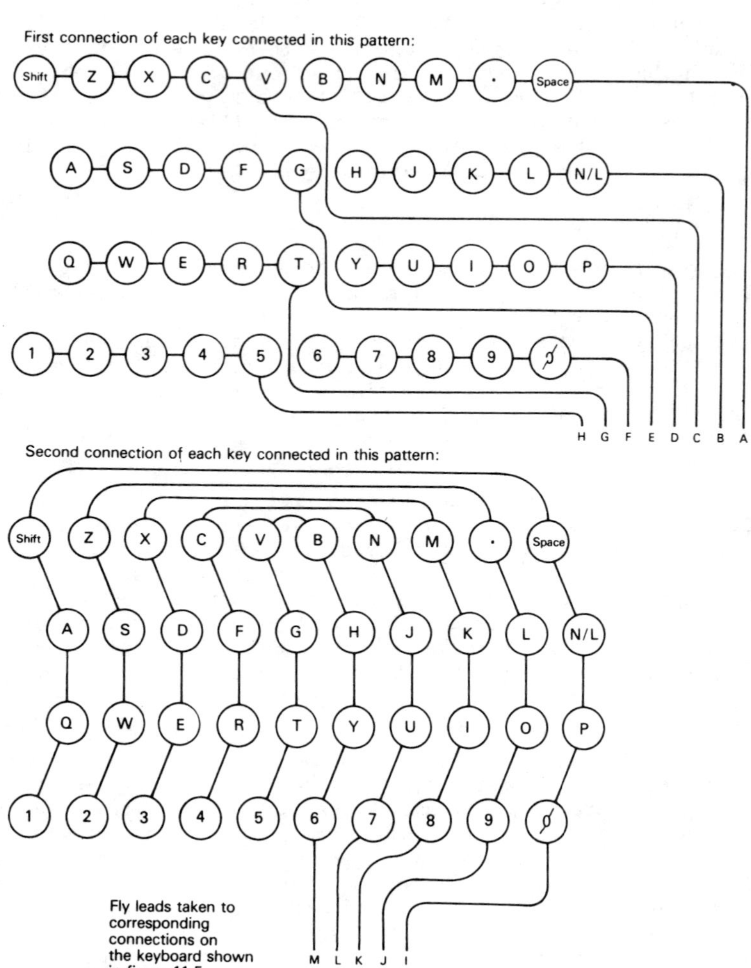

Figure 11.4 Underside of the keyboard and interconnection of the keys

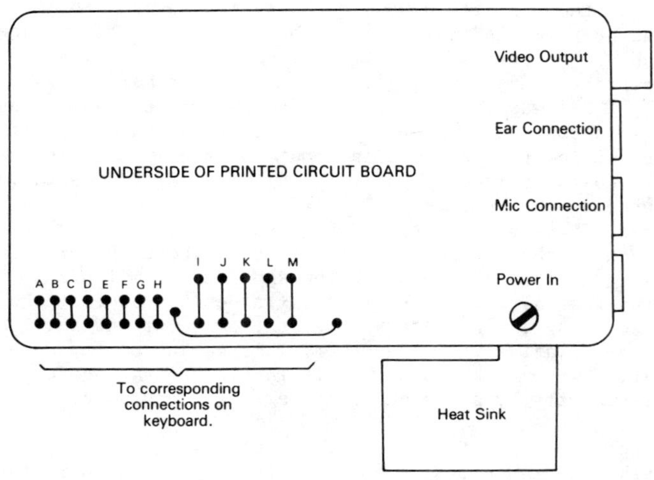

Figure 11.5 Linking the ZX81 to a normal keyboard

This is the largest project in the chapter and the wiring will take some time to complete and will need careful checking. The cost is likely to be low and, as the likelihood of damage to the equipment is very small; don't be put off. The computer will remain available during the project as the bulk of the work is done on the keyboard alone. When attaching the leads to the computer some important precautions must be taken. The chips will not take kindly to being blasted with AC, even the small amount that leaks from a grounded iron. The safest plan is to heat the iron thoroughly and then switch off both the computer and the iron before attempting a joint. The tinned leads can be quickly soldered in place before the iron cools and the iron can be soon brought back to temperature between each lead. This sounds more involved than it really is. There are only thirteen leads to solder. Alternatively, use a ceramic-shafted iron.

Re-designating the keys is a job that can be off-loaded onto an artistic friend. The job consists of filling the recess of each key (they are usually concave) with something like car body filler, sanding this smooth and priming it in some way to receive the ink drawing of the key characters and finally, sealing with a durable, transparent film. The self adhesive Sinclair keyboard can be cut up and used but the area of adhesive is small and the characters tend to move around on the keys and look untidy.

ELIMINATING THE TANGLE

Even with the plasticine pad in place, I have had problems when a lead has been joggled while I have been sorting through papers on the table. The cure was a little elaborate but resulted in a much more professional looking set up and no further program losses. The ZX81 was stripped out of its plastic box and mounted securely in a case built on the pattern of an executive brief case. The deck of the case was laid out to take my tape recorder and the keyboard, tilted slightly forward for more comfortable typing. Underneath the deck all the wiring was soldered in place, not plugged. The most important job of this type was to solder the 16K RAM pack to the printed circuit board of the computer using ribbon cable. This meant removing the RAM pack from its case, opening out the two halves to make it lie flat on the base of the case, and then securing it in place so that the computer and the memory did not move relative to one another. This was necessary because the soldering was "tack" soldering to the top of the board to very small areas of strip, and such joints are not very robust.

It is not necessary to go to such lengths if you don't feel up to the task. The RAM pack can be connected to the board in the normal way in the box and secured in place to avoid the memory-losing joggling. The main benefit of the case is the lack of tangle and the more orderly nature of the computing area, which is conducive to more ordered programming.

USING THE 'WORD JUGGLER' PROGRAM

TO WRITE TEXT

Key 1 followed by NEWLINE to select "write" mode. When you have entered 32 characters the screen will blank for a short while before the cursor appears on the next line. It is during this blank period that the text is copied into the memory.

TO RETURN TO THE MAIN MENU

Key Q while holding the shift key down. Note that you cannot return directly to the menu from "edit" mode.

TO MOVE BETWEEN 'EDIT' AND 'WRITE' MODES

Key M while holding the shift key down.

TO EDIT

Use the cursor controls (arrows) but *without* shift. Note that the 'up' arrow moves the cursor up a complete paragraph at a time whereas the 'down' arrow moves the cursor down one line. To return to the menu from "edit" mode, you must first go to "write" mode by keying shift/M.

TO FILE TEXT ON TAPE

Select "file text" from the menu by keying 5 then NEWLINE. Start the recorder (set to record) and after a few seconds to allow the motor speed to stabilise, key NEWLINE again. Word Juggler will return to the menu when recording is complete. Stop the recorder. Make a backup copy if you wish by repeating the operation.

TO PRINT TEXT

Select this option from the menu by keying 6 and then NEWLINE. The computer will ask for the number of the last paragraph to be printed - everything from the beginning of the text to this point will be printed out. Enter the number and key NEWLINE. When the screen displays 'finished', key NEWLINE to return to the menu.

TO READ TEXT

Select this option from the menu by keying 3 then NEWLINE. Press NEWLINE repeatedly (or hold it down) to step through the text. At the end of the text the program will return to the menu.

TO DELETE PARAGRAPHS

Select this option by keying 4 and then NEWLINE. You will be asked which paragraph you want to delete. Enter the paragraph number, followed by NEWLINE. You have to confirm the deletion by keying D followed by NEWLINE. The screen will blank for a while. You can delete successive paragraphs by keying D followed by NEWLINE again. *REMEMBER* to return to the menu at least once every 18 paragraphs to avoid crashing the program with a screen full of messages.

TO RESTART THE PROGRAM

If for any reason you crash Word Juggler (e.g. by keying "break") and it returns to the listing, restart by keying GOTO 3000 followed by NEWLINE.

USING THE PROGRAM AS LOADED FROM THE MACMILLAN CASSETTE TAPE

The "WORD 1" package doubles as a tape catalogue. To read the catalogue, simply key 3 followed by NEWLINE to select "read" mode from the menu. Then key NEWLINE again for each successive page. To exit from "read" mode, hold down NEWLINE until the menu returns.

The program needs a minor change for use as a word processor. Select "delete" by keying 4 followed by NEWLINE. Delete paragraphs up to paragraph 32, beginning at paragraph 0. Exit from "delete" mode by keying NEWLINE. ***REMEMBER*** to return to the menu at paragraph 16 to clear the screen of messages.

Finally, key 3 from the main menu, followed by NEWLINE. Then key BREAK. The program will stop with report code D/3520. Enter as a direct command:

```
3500 LET P=2   then NEWLINE
GOTO 3000      then NEWLINE
```

...which gets you back to the main menu.

☐ Yes, send me your free catalog, BRAINFOOD, which lists over 80 microcomputer books covering software, hardware, business applications, general computer literacy and programming languages.

I understand that you will give me $1 off my next order when I order from BRAINFOOD.

$1 OFF NEXT ORDER!

NAME ______________________________

ADDRESS ______________________________

CITY, STATE, ZIP ______________________________

☐ Yes, send me your free catalog, BRAINFOOD, which lists over 80 microcomputer books covering software, hardware, business applications, general computer literacy and programming languages.

I understand that you will give me $1 off my next order when I order from BRAINFOOD.

$1 OFF NEXT ORDER!

NAME ______________________________

ADDRESS ______________________________

CITY, STATE, ZIP ______________________________

☐ Yes, send me your free catalog, BRAINFOOD, which lists over 80 microcomputer books covering software, hardware, business applications, general computer literacy and programming languages.

I understand that you will give me $1 off my next order when I order from BRAINFOOD.

$1 OFF NEXT ORDER!

NAME ______________________________

ADDRESS ______________________________

CITY, STATE, ZIP ______________________________

FREE CATALOG FREE
CATALOG FREE CATA
LOG FREE CATALOG
FREE CATALOG FREE
CATALOG FREE CATA
LOG FREE CATALOG
FREE CATALOG FREE
CATALOG FREE CATA
LOG FREE CATALOG
FREE CATALOG FREE
CATALOG FREE CATA
LOG FREE CATALOG
FREE CATALOG FREE
CATALOG FREE CATA
LOG FREE CATALOG
FREE CATALOG FREE
CATALOG FREE CATA
LOG FREE CATALOG
FREE CATALOG FREE
CATALOG FREE CATA
LOG FREE CATALOG
FREE CATALOG FREE
CATALOG FREE CATA
LOG FREE CATALOG

Mail To:

dilithium Press
P.O. Box E
Beaverton, OR 97075

Or Call:

800-547-1842

FREE CATALOG FREE
CATALOG FREE CATA
LOG FREE CATALOG
FREE CATALOG FREE
CATALOG FREE CATA
LOG FREE CATALOG
FREE CATALOG FREE
CATALOG FREE CATA
LOG FREE CATALOG
FREE CATALOG FREE
CATALOG FREE CATA
LOG FREE CATALOG
FREE CATALOG FREE
CATALOG FREE CATA
LOG FREE CATALOG
FREE CATALOG FREE
CATALOG FREE CATA
LOG FREE CATALOG
FREE CATALOG FREE
CATALOG FREE CATA
LOG FREE CATALOG
FREE CATALOG FREE
CATALOG FREE CATA
LOG FREE CATALOG
FREE CATALOG FREE

NO POSTAGE
NECESSARY
IF MAILED
IN THE
UNITED STATES

BUSINESS REPLY CARD

FIRST CLASS PERMIT NO. 143 BEAVERTON, OREGON

POSTAGE WILL BE PAID BY ADDRESSEE

dilithium Software

P.O. Box 606
Beaverton, OR 97075